easy outdoor living

easy outdoor living
40 great garden projects

Clare Matthews
photographs by **Clive Nichols**

hamlyn

For 'The Girls': Judith, Linzi,
Surita, Kate, Louise and Liz.

First published in Great Britain
in 2007 by Hamlyn, a division of
Octopus Publishing Group Ltd
2-4 Heron Quays, London E14 4JP

ISBN-13: 978-0-60061-521-7
ISBN-10: 0-600-61521-9

A CIP catalogue record for this book is available
from the British Library

Printed and bound in China

10 9 8 7 6 5 4 3 2 1

The author and publisher have made every effort to
ensure that all instructions and ideas given in this
book are accurate and safe, but they cannot accept
liability for any injury, damage or loss to either person
or the property whether direct or consequential and
howsoever arising.

Measurements
Both imperial and metric measurements have been
given throughout this book. When following
instructions, you should choose to work in either
metric or imperial, and never mix the two.

contents

introduction

Ask most people what they want from their gardens and it will be versatile outdoor space – an extension of their homes, well designed and well equipped to allow activities to flow seamlessly from inside to outside. For most the garden is a space associated with the better things in life, where the emphasis is on relaxation and recreation. Few want to spend hours working the soil and tending a multitude of demanding plants; rather we desire an easily maintained garden, brimming with easy-going planting and perhaps a few veg. In short, a garden boasting all we need to relax, play, entertain friends, barbecue or dine in style, and spend time with the family.

This book is not about redesigning the structure of your garden but about creating stylish, unusual and functional objects to improve the outdoor living space you have. Divided into five parts, it looks at all aspects of outdoor living and shows with simple step-by-step instructions how to make innovative and practical furnishings and features, each aimed at making time spent in the garden more enjoyable and rewarding for all the family. Each chapter also boasts a wealth of quick and easy ideas and tips to boost your garden's appeal and enrich your life outdoors.

In addition to the materials listed with each project the following equipment is needed for constructing the outdoor living ideas in this book:

General
Pencil, pen, felt pen
Ruler
Scissors
Tape measure
Sponge
Soft cloth
Card
String
Pins
Matches or lighter
Plates, coins, cups
   etc. to use as
   templates

Tin snips
Sandpaper
Paintbrushes

Gardening projects
Spade
Trowel
Watering can
Turf cutter
Wire cutters
Hose or rope

Sewing projects
Sewing machine
Needles
Dressmaker's pins
Dressmaker's
   scissors

DIY projects
Drill and drill bits
   of various sizes
Jigsaw
Handsaw
Hammer
Rubber mallet
Large nail
Screwdriver
Spirit level

al fresco dining

Every outdoor space needs the basics for al fresco dining: an area of paving or decking with a simple table and chairs, the dimensions dictated by space, family size and budget. Beyond this are a myriad of options to make eating outdoors easier and a real pleasure. If you have the space, think of equipping two areas for eating. As

well as the obvious, practical terrace, you might create a less formal area away from the house for meals with the more carefree mood of a picnic. You will undoubtedly use the garden more for everyday dining if everything you need is set up and readily to hand, so work towards this with robust, easily cared for furnishings, and save delicate or labour-intensive features to mark celebrations or occasions when the extra effort will make them really special. Whether a quick lunchtime snack for one, a romantic dinner for two or a stylish supper for ten, your garden can provide the perfect setting.

sari canopy

Draped across a quickly erected, simple structure, a richly decorated sari defines an extraordinary, intimate dining space. The sari canopy provides shade, shelter, seclusion and boundaries within which a decadent dining escape can be built. If you prefer, the sari can be replaced with a length of any sumptuous or colourful fabric.

skill level **1**

time **2 hours**

you will need:

4 x 1 m (3 ft) lengths of dowel

2 x 2 m (6 ft) lengths of dowel

silver spray paint

about 18 m (20 yd) nylon cord

6 tent pegs

1 sari, or fabric about 6 m x 120 cm (6 yd x 48 in)

6 clip curtain rings

1 Mark a point 18 cm (7 in) from one end of each piece of dowel and, using a 4 mm (⅛ in) bit, drill a hole at each point.

2 Use the silver spray paint to apply a coat of paint to each of the dowels. Leave to dry.

3 Drive the tallest pair of dowels into the ground the same distance apart as the sari or fabric is wide and thread a length of cord through the holes in both, tying a knot both sides of the hole so that the cord between the posts is taut. Pull the free ends of the cord out from the posts like the guy ropes of a tent and secure them with the tent pegs.

4

5

4 Repeat this process with the two shorter pairs of dowels, spaced so that your fabric stretches across all the uprights and just touches the ground.

5 The canopy structure should be completely solid. If not, try tightening the guy ropes and driving the posts further into the ground.

6 Finally, drape the fabric across the structure. Once it is hanging evenly secure the sari to the cords with clip curtain rings.

6

picnic box

Lined with fresh, checked fabric and equipped with everything you need for al fresco dining, this robust box makes laying the table outside an easy matter. You can assemble whatever dining sundries you wish, but here are plates, bowls, cutlery, napkins, citronella candles, glasses, a cruet, corkscrew and even a bottle of wine, all held securely by elastic straps. Kept well stocked the holdall is great for country picnics and the beach too.

skill level **1**

time **2 hours**

you will need:

1 wooden wine case

4 m (12 ft) hardy hemp rope, 25 mm (1 in) diameter

about 1 m (1 yd) fabric (depending on the size of your box)

masking tape

brass-headed upholstery tacks

plates, bowls etc.

3 small terracotta pots

elastic, 1.5 cm (¾ in) wide

1 First make the handles. Using a 25 mm (1 in) bit, drill a hole on each face of the box, close to the corners (see picture). Thread a length of rope through each set of holes and tie overhand knots to hold them in position. Allow the ends to fray – it looks good.

2 Now line the wine box with the fabric. Drape about 6 cm (2½ in) over the side of the box and fold under the edges to give a neat finish. Fold the fabric neatly on itself at the corners. Use masking tape to hold it in place as you work around the box.

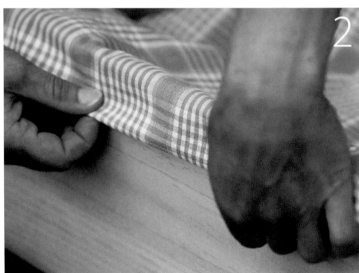

3 When you are happy with the position of the lining tap in upholstery tacks along the folded edge at regular intervals to hold the lining in place.

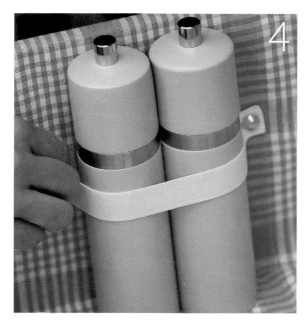

4 Now arrange the items you have chosen to include in the box to achieve the best fit and weight distribution. The holdall will be much easier to carry if it is well balanced. Fold over one end of the elastic and tack it into position, stretch the elastic around each object so it is held securely and cut, fold and tack the other end of the elastic.

5 Terracotta pots make apt holders for any loose items like cutlery and napkins.

6 Plates and bowls are best held by criss-crossed elastic in the base of the box. Pack all your items into the holdall and it is ready for use.

skill level **1**

time **30 mins**

you will need:

1 or more galvanized
buckets

paving stones or similar
heatproof surface

charcoal

firelighters

grill rack

barbecue buckets

Cooking good food outdoors need not require masses of shiny, expensive equipment. A galvanized bucket, suitably adapted, makes a stylish and efficient barbecue, and a bank of barbecue buckets makes catering for large parties easy. It also means you can cook vegetarian food and tempting puddings on their own buckets, away from fish and meat. An array of buckets set along a stable bench or table have a utilitarian chic and enough cooking surface for a large gathering but are inexpensive and easily stacked and stowed away after the event. A single bucket is also great for picnics; it is easy to carry and can be used to transport picnic paraphernalia before it is unpacked and lit.

1 Using a large stout nail and a hammer puncture holes around the base of each bucket about 2–3 cm (1 in) up from its base.

2 Set each bucket on a non-combustible, heatproof base or on a paving stone. To bring the grill surface up to a comfortable height we improvised a cooking bench with a broad plank set on large terracotta pots.

3 Add a layer of charcoal and tuck in some firelighters.

4 Light the barbecue in the usual way and wait until the coals are hot enough to start cooking.

5 When the coals are glowing red, set the grill on top of the bucket and you are ready to cook.

Playing with fire

Barbecues are tremendous fun for all the family, but don't overlook a few basic safety measures. Before you light it, ensure your barbecue base is very stable, so it can't tip over if jogged. Make sure the bucket itself is sitting on a fireproof surface and not in contact with anything that can scorch or catch fire. Always use oven gloves when barbecuing as the buckets will become very hot. Over-excited young children (and pets) won't always look where they are going, so don't let them race around near the cooking area. Have a fire blanket to hand, and don't leave matches or lighters lying around for children to pick up.

easy barbecue recipes

Good, simple food best suits the relaxed mood of dining in the garden; food that can be effortlessly prepared outdoors or easily carried to the table. Reliable recipes that look and taste delicious yet allow the cook to be as carefree as the guests are essential. With minimum preparation for impressive results, these dishes are ideally suited to al fresco dining.

WATERMELON AND FETA SALAD

Preparation time 10 mins **Cooking time** 5 mins **Serves** 4

1 tablespoon black sesame seeds
500 g (1 lb) watermelon, peeled and diced
175 g (6 oz) feta cheese, diced
50 g (2 oz) rocket leaves
a few mint, parsley and coriander sprigs
6 tablespoons extra virgin olive oil
1 tablespoon orange flower water
1¹/₂ tablespoons lemon juice
1 teaspoon pomegranate syrup (optional)
¹/₂ teaspoon sugar
salt and pepper
toasted pitta bread, to serve

1 Dry-fry the sesame seeds for a few minutes until aromatic, then set aside.

2 Arrange the watermelon and feta on a large plate with the rocket and herbs.

3 Whisk together the olive oil, orange flower water, lemon juice, pomegranate syrup, if using, and sugar, then season to taste with salt and pepper and drizzle over the salad. Scatter over the sesame seeds and serve with toasted pitta bread.

MUSHROOM PARCELS WITH MELTING CHEESE

Preparation time 12–15 mins **Cooking time** 15 mins **Serves** 4

12 flat mushrooms
2 garlic cloves, crushed
1 teaspoon chopped thyme
dash lemon juice
125 g (4 oz) softened butter
50 g (2 oz) Pecorino cheese, grated
salt and pepper
crusty bread, to serve

1 Divide the mushrooms between 4 large pieces of foil. Beat the garlic, thyme and lemon juice into the butter and season to taste with salt and pepper. Dot the flavoured butter over the mushrooms.

2 Seal the foil to form parcels and cook over hot coals or in a preheated oven, 200°C (400°F), Gas Mark 6, for 10–15 minutes.

3 Open the parcels, sprinkle over the cheese and allow to melt slightly, then serve with crusty bread.

CLASSIC AMERICAN BURGER

Preparation time 15 minutes, plus chilling
Cooking time 15 minutes **Serves** 4

1 kg (2 lb) good quality coarsely minced beef
2 garlic cloves, crushed
8 streaky bacon rashers
a little light olive oil, for brushing
salt and pepper

TO SERVE
4 large burger buns
75 g (3 oz) mixed salad leaves
1 beef tomato, sliced
4 thick slices strong Cheddar cheese or Monterey Jack
1 small red onion, sliced into rings
1 quantity of Quick BBQ Sauce

1 Mix the beef and garlic together and season well with salt and pepper. Divide the mixture into 4 equal portions and form each one into a round patty, pressing together firmly. Cover and chill for at least 30 minutes.

2 Grill the bacon until slightly crisp and keep it warm. Heat a griddle pan or barbecue to medium-high. Brush the burgers with a little oil and cook them for 5–6 minutes on each side, depending on how you like them cooked.

3 Assemble each burger by covering the base of each bun first with salad leaves, then tomato slices. Place the cooked burger on the salad, then top with the cheese, bacon and sliced red onion. Serve open or topped with the bun lid and accompanied with the quick BBQ sauce.

QUICK BBQ SAUCE

Preparation time 5 minutes
Cooking time 5–10 minutes **Makes** 450 ml (¾ pint)

250 ml (8 fl oz) tomato ketchup
125 ml (4 fl oz) tomato purée
125 ml (4 fl oz) apple cider vinegar
4 tablespoons blackstrap molasses or black treacle
1 tablespoon Worcestershire sauce
1 teaspoon Dijon mustard
1 teaspoon Tabasco sauce (or Chipotle Tabasco)

1 Place all the ingredients in a saucepan and simmer over a medium heat for 5–10 minutes or until thick.

2 Pour into sterilized jars and leave to cool. Use immediately or store in the refrigerator for up to 2 weeks.

SALT-CRUSTED PRAWNS WITH CHILLI JAM

Preparation time 10 mins **Cooking time** 20 mins **Serves** 4

12 large raw tiger prawns in their shells
1 tablespoon olive oil
50 g (2 oz) sea salt
lemon wedges, to garnish

CHILLI JAM
4 ripe tomatoes
½ red onion
2 red chillies
2 tablespoons dark soy sauce
2 tablespoons clear honey
salt and pepper

1 First make the chilli jam. Roughly chop the tomatoes, onion and chillies. Place in a food processor with the soy sauce and honey, season to taste with salt and pepper and process until smooth.

2 Transfer the jam to a saucepan and bring to the boil. Simmer rapidly for 15 minutes, until thickened. Plunge the pan into iced water and leave to cool.

3 Meanwhile, carefully cut along the back of the prawns with a small pair of scissors and pull out the black vein. Wash and dry well on kitchen paper.

4 Toss the prawns with the oil and then coat thoroughly with salt. Cook the prawns in their salt jackets over hot coals or in a heated griddle pan for 2–3 minutes on each side. Serve with the chilli jam and lemon wedges to garnish.

BARBECUED FRUITS WITH PALM SUGAR

Preparation time 10 mins, plus cooling
Cooking time 6–8 mins **Serves** 4

25 g (1 oz) palm sugar
grated rind and juice of 1 lime
2 tablespoons water
½ teaspoon cracked black peppercorns
500 g (1 lb) mixed prepared fruits (such as pineapple slices, mango wedges and peaches)

TO SERVE
cinnamon or vanilla ice cream
lime slices

1 Warm the sugar, lime rind and juice, water and peppercorns in a small pan until the sugar has dissolved. Plunge the base of the pan into iced water to cool.

2 Brush the cooled syrup over the prepared fruits and barbecue or grill for 3–4 minutes on each side until they are charred and tender. Serve with scoops of cinnamon or vanilla ice cream and slices of lime.

criss-cross table
and chairs

A remarkable table and chairs that can be made in an instant but will last for years. This colourful furniture, simple, stable and deceptively comfortable, can be moved around the garden to create inviting, informal seating areas throughout the summer and then can be stowed tidily away for the winter months.

skill level 3

time 2 hours

you will need:

planed wood
25 mm (1 in) depth x
265 mm (10 in) width

for each chair:
1 x 1.1 m (43 in) length
and 1 x 80 cm (32 in)
length

for the table:
2 x 65 cm (26 in) lengths
and 1 x 37 cm (15 in)
length

preservative wood stain

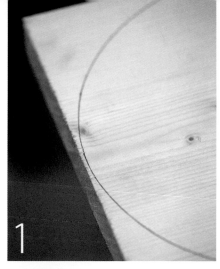

To make a chair

1 Using a dinner plate as a template, draw a curve at one end of each piece of wood.

2 Cut around the curves with a jigsaw and thoroughly sand any rough edges.

3 On both pieces of wood mark a point 30 cm (12 in) from the square end and another 25 mm (1 in) from the first. From each point draw a straight line exactly halfway in to the centre of the plank. Join these two parallel lines to form the dimensions of the slot. Using a jigsaw once again, cut out the slots. Sand any rough edges.

4 Apply two coats of preservative wood stain and, when dry, slot the chair together.

To make the table

5 Follow the same method as described for Step 3 of the chair, and cut a slot 35 cm (13½ in) from one end of each of the 65 cm (26 in) lengths of wood. Slot the two pieces of wood together so they form a cross. Cut a 45-degree angle on the two cut edges of the remaining piece of wood to form the tabletop. Drop it into position in the top of the cross.

6 Take the table apart, apply two coats of preservative wood stain to all faces of the wood and when it is dry slot the table together again.

fabric chair cover

Weathered garden furniture can be appealing, but perhaps not when you are planning a smart al fresco meal. A quick and inexpensive solution is to disguise the chairs in crisp, fresh sheeting and deck them with bows, ribbons and posies. Choose colours to match your table linen and add flowers or leaves on ribbons to the chair backs.

skill level 1

time 15 mins per chair

you will need:

cotton sheeting
(see Step 1 for calculating
amount)

fabric glue

2¹/₂–3 m (2¹/₂ yd) polyester
voile for each chair

flowers for posy decoration

ribbon in toning or
complementary colour

1 Measure for a piece of sheeting long enough to go from the ground on one side of the chair over the seat and to the floor on the other, allowing for a 2 cm (¾ in) turning at each end.

2 Do the same from the ground over the back of the chair, down over the seat and to the floor again. The width will depend on the dimensions of your chairs, but be generous with the fabric to ensure the chair will be hidden. Cut our your sheeting lengths and use fabric glue to secure the hems.

3 Drape the first piece of fabric across the seat ensuring it is even both sides. Add the second piece of fabric up and over the back of the chair, once again ensuring it is correctly placed. Depending on the shape of your chairs it may be necessary to use some pins to hold the fabric.

4 Cut a length of voile and tie it around the chair back, finishing it with a large bow.

5 Tie flowers (we used lavender and marguerites) into a posy with a length of ribbon and tie the posy to the centre of the voile bow.

quick and easy cocktails

Give a gathering certain trappings and it becomes an extra-special affair. Attention to detail in table decorations, linen, lighting and menu all contribute, but a selection of well-chosen drinks and cocktails will really help any event get off to an impressive start and lift the spirits. Fortunately beautiful, glamorous-sounding cocktails are surprisingly straightforward to make.

PINK MOJITO Serves 1

½ lime
6–8 mint leaves
2 teaspoons sugar syrup
3 raspberries
crushed ice
2 measures white rum
½ measure Chambord
dash cranberry juice
mint sprig, to decorate

Combine the first 4 ingredients in the base of a highball glass and add a scoop of crushed ice. Add the rum and stir, then add the Chambord and top with the cranberry juice. Finally, decorate with a mint sprig.

TANGERINE CHILL Serves 6

ice cubes
6 measures light rum
4 measures Cointreau
8 measures tangerine juice
8 measures fresh pink grapefruit juice
2 measures fresh lime juice
2 measures cherry juice
1 measure fresh lemon juice
sugar syrup, to taste
lime and lemon twists, to decorate

Put plenty of ice cubes in a large jug. Pour over the rum, Cointreau and fruit juices and stir well. Add sugar syrup to taste. Serve in punch glasses, decorated with lime and lemon twists, and keep chilled at all times with ice cubes.

CAMPITO Serves 1

3 lime wedges
2 orange wedges
6–8 mint leaves
2 teaspoons sugar
dash passion fruit syrup
crushed ice
2 measures gold rum
½ measure Campari
dash soda water
red berries, to decorate

Combine the first 5 ingredients in the base of a highball glass and add a scoop of crushed ice. Add the rum, then the Campari, stirring after each addition, then add a little more crushed ice and top with soda water. Finally, decorate with red berries.

PIMM'S COCKTAIL Serves 6

ice cubes
6 measures Pimm's No 1
4 measures gin
750 ml (1¼ pints) ginger ale
300 ml (½ pint) lemonade
1 lime, segmented
blueberries, strawberries and strips of cucumber
mint sprig, to decorate

Put plenty of ice cubes in a large jug. Build all the liquid ingredients over the ice, add all the fruit and strips of cucumber and stir until thoroughly chilled. Serve in ice-filled tumblers, decorated with sprigs of mint.

SANGRIA BLANCO Serves 6

ice cubes
4 measures citron-flavoured vodka
2 measures peach schnapps
2 measures white peach purée
1 measure fresh lemon juice
500 ml (17 fl oz) dry white wine
1 litre (1³/₄ pints) fresh apple juice, to top up
apple and lemon slices, to decorate

Prepare well in advance of serving. Put plenty of ice cubes in a large jug and pour over all the ingredients. Stir regularly as the cocktail chills. Serve over ice cubes in goblets, decorated with apple and lemon slices.

ORCHARD BREEZE Serves 6

ice cubes
8 measures vodka
2 measures elderflower cordial
8 measures dry white wine
1 measure fresh lime juice
12 measures fresh apple juice
325 ml (11 fl oz) lemonade, to top up
white grapes, apple slices and lime wedges, to decorate

Fill a large jug with ice cubes and pour over all the ingredients. Stir well. Add grapes, apple slices and lime wedges to decorate. Serve in ice-filled punch glasses or cups.

BAY BREEZE Serves 6

ice cubes
8 measures vodka
750 ml (1¼ pints) cranberry juice
350 ml (12 fl oz) pineapple juice
lime wedges, to decorate

Fill a large jug with ice cubes and pour over all the ingredients. Stir well. Add lime wedges to decorate. Serve in ice-filled highball glasses.

low sleeper table

Reclining on luxurious, plump cushions heaped around a low table is a relaxed way to dine; this robust table is the perfect height for just such a decadent set-up. Fashioned from chunks of wood, the table will last for years and is equally suited to more everyday use in front of a bench. This is a rugged table made of unplaned wooden sleepers, but you could use planed timber for a sleeker look.

skill level **2**

time **2 hours**

you will need:

2 x 1.8 m (6 ft) lengths of new sleepers or wood, 12 x 20 cm (5 x 8 in)

1.2 m (4 ft) dowel, 20 mm (¾ in) diameter, cut into 20 cm (8 in) lengths

exterior wood glue

1 First cut the wood to size. Measure and cut three 90 cm (3 ft) lengths and two 45 cm (18 in) lengths. Your timber supplier may do this for you. Now mark two points on each of the three longer pieces halfway across the width and 25 cm (10 in) in from either end. Use a 20 mm (¾ in) drill bit to make a hole 10 cm (4 in) deep at each point.

2 On each of the two shorter pieces mark three points along the centre of their length, at the mid-point and 2.5 cm (1 in) in from either end. Drill holes the same size and depth as on the longer pieces.

3 Coat one half of each dowel with glue and push them firmly into the three holes in each of the shorter lengths. Allow the glue to dry. Now spread glue on the protruding dowels and lower the sleepers that form the tabletop into position. Ensure the ends of the sleepers form a straight edge and leave the glue to dry.

QUICK & EASY IDEAS

LEFT An edible flower encased in an ice cube not only keeps summer drinks cool but makes them pretty too. Violas, scented geraniums, nasturtiums and calendula flowers all work well, adding a dash of colour to all kinds of drinks. Fill the ice tray as normal, push a washed flower head or a few petals under the surface of the water of each cube and freeze.

ABOVE and LEFT This flowery tea-light holder made of ice is especially appealing. Choose two plastic vessels, one 3 or 4 cm (about 1½ in) smaller than the other, put ice cubes in the bottom of the larger one and sit the smaller on them. Fill both with water and cram flowers into the water between the two. Put the whole thing into the freezer overnight. To remove the ice light from its mould run it under a little warm water. Then just add a small candle.

LEFT If you are looking to create a special mood and your table linen just isn't right, a sheet or two of elaborately painted or hand-made wrapping paper placed at the centre of the table add a touch of pizzazz.

RIGHT On bright but breezy days keeping the cloth on the table can be difficult, but this glitzy tablecloth weight will help keep things where they should be. Any small but weighty object can be wired on to ring curtain clips – shells, pebbles, fir cones or a cluster of beads would all do the job well.

RIGHT Arranging a show-stopping centrepiece for a table outdoors does not have to be difficult or complex. Choose a collection of plants in bloom – shrubs, perennials or annuals, whatever looks good at that moment. Choose flowers united by a strong colour theme. Wrap their pots in matching scraps of fabric and ribbons and group them at the centre of the table. Once the celebration is over the plants can be planted out in the garden or in permanent containers, making them a much thriftier option than cut flowers.

QUICK & EASY IDEAS

RIGHT Snipped from the garden, a flexible sprig of fresh rosemary looped around a portly pillar candle is just enough to dress it for the table. Lengths of climbing plants such as golden hop (*Humulus lupulus*) or clematis or even fern fronds could be used just as effectively.

ABOVE Simple but not plain: a pliable stem of rosemary wound around a napkin takes only a moment to do but looks great.

RIGHT For a contemporary look decorate your table with spiky cacti in ceramic pots. Happy outside in most climates for the summer, plump cacti can stay on the table all season, their beauty on constant display, and can then spend the cooler part of the year inside.

Using a few flowers and leaves from the garden to add a flourish to the table when dining outdoors is particularly appropriate and an inexpensive 'quick fix'. 'Natural' napkin rings are especially easy to make to decorate the place of each guest, and place cards can even be tucked into the ring.

RIGHT A bold gerbera, held in place with florist's wire, is a simple but confident decoration, making a splash on subdued linen.

ABOVE Raffia and a sunshine yellow flowerhead of achillea tie cutlery and napkin neatly together.

RIGHT Tucked into a modest ribbon tied into a bow a few snippets of lavender make a fragrant, attractive napkin decoration.

relaxation
and escape

Most of us see our gardens, however humble, as an escape from the hectic pace and demands of everyday life. Making your garden a haven for relaxation is about shutting out the world beyond and constructing your own secluded paradise, whatever that may mean for you. A hammock and a good book in a  shady, quiet corner may be enough, or you may need to build up more physical barriers and cocoons to shelter yourself from the world outside. A comfortable place to rest and soothing sounds and smells will help to engender a magical, hazy tranquillity. The projects in this chapter will help you to create your ideal space, somewhere that exudes peace and serenity, where the hubbub of real life is kept at bay, at least for a while.

no-sew hammock

There is nothing quite so relaxing as snoozing in a gently swaying hammock. Brightly coloured and hardwearing, this hammock has the added advantage of looking great too. Made from heavy-duty upholstery fabric, it requires no sewing and takes little time to put together.

skill level 1

time 1 hour 30 mins

you will need:

2 m x 2 m (2 yd x 2 yd) heavy-duty upholstery fabric

14 x 2 cm (¾ in) eyelets

about 8 m (25 ft) hardy hemp rope 8 mm (⅓ in) diameter, cut in half (length required will vary according to where you sling the hammock)

1 Fold the fabric in half lengthways, using pins to hold it in place.

2 At both ends of the length of fabric fold over 4 cm (1½ in) of material and then fold it over again. Secure the folded hem with pins.

3 Using the device supplied with the eyelets secure them at 8 cm (3 in) intervals along the hem, through all the layers of fabric. Remove all of the pins once all the eyelets have been secured.

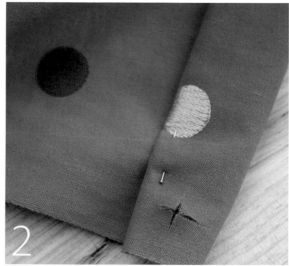

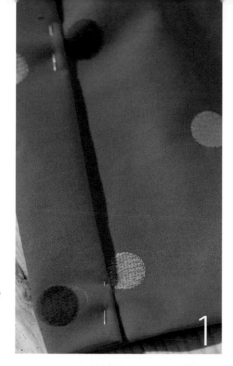

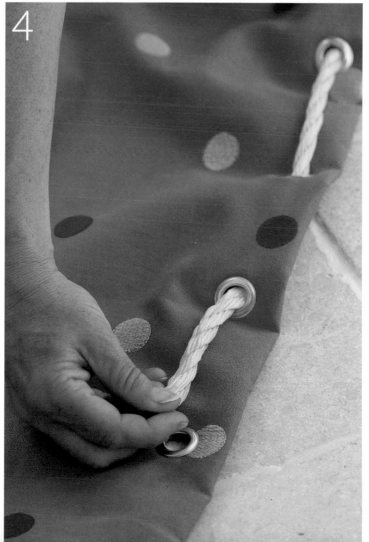

Safety
Always ensure the supports you choose are sufficiently sturdy for sustained load-bearing.

4 Finally, take one piece of rope and weave it in and out of the eyelets at one end of the hammock. Pull it through so the hammock sling is at the centre of the length of rope. Repeat this at the other end of the hammock with the second piece of rope. The hammock is now ready to tie in position.

rope screen hideaway

skill level **2**

time **5 hours**

you will need:

6 cm (2½ in) diameter round posts: 8 x 1.5 m (5 ft) lengths and 1 x 1 m (3 ft) length (or other combination to provide the cut lengths listed in Step 1)

60 m (65 yd) synthetic hardy hemp rope, 16 mm (⅝ in) diameter

20 mm (¾ in) screws

8 mm (⅓ in) sisal rope (length will depend on how dense you wish your screen to be)

driftwood and shells

Redolent of the beach and the spirit of seaside holidays, this secluded woven rope nook is the perfect addition to a garden lacking a quiet corner or private hideaway. The screen is constructed from rope and rough timber, which will mellow and improve with age. This hideaway is designed for just one or two people, but there is no reason why the structure should not be stretched to accommodate a table and chairs if needed.

1 First cut the posts to size. You will need, in order from left to right across the screen, 11 posts, arranged with their dimensions in the following order: 60, 70, 80, 90, 110, 120, 135, 150, 135, 115 and 90 cm (24, 28, 32, 36, 44, 48, 54, 60, 54, 46 and 36 in). These lengths are suggestions, and assume you are able to drive the posts about 20 cm (8 in) into the ground. You may need to adjust the measurements according to your ground conditions and post lengths available. Mark out the curve of the screen on the ground with a tape measure, so it is 6 m (20 ft) in length. Take time to stand back and adjust the line – aim for an unfinished oval shape.

2 Lay out the posts at 60 cm (2 ft) intervals along the curve of the tape, following the order in Step 1, so that the shortest is at one end and the height gradually increases towards the middle back of the screen before decreasing again. Drive each post into the ground so it is held firmly and the height difference between it and its neighbour is preserved.

3 Starting at the shortest post, attach the end of the hemp rope to the post with a screw.

4 Weave the rope in and out of the posts, pulling the rope taut and screwing it to the posts where necessary.

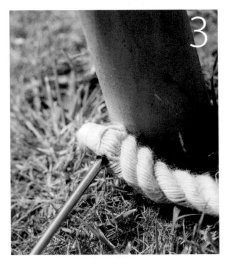

5 Wind the rope back and forth, working in a curve to echo the top of the posts. Space the ropes to form a screen that creates privacy but still lets through some light. To finish off, screw the other end of the rope to the post to hold it in place.

6 Now weave through lengths of sisal rope up and down through the rope warp, tying it at the bottom and leaving the ends long. Add as many weft ropes as you desire. Finally, decorate the rope screen with shells and driftwood.

Tip
The sisal looks attractive with frayed ends, but the hemp rope should be kept intact. To stop it unravelling, bind both ends and use a naked flame to seal them.

hanging deckchair

Extremely comfortable and irresistibly inviting, this hanging deckchair is incredibly easy to construct, but is deceptively robust. As it is more upright than a standard hammock the chair is the perfect location to savour the small pleasures of a good book or a cup of tea.

skill level **2**

time **3 hours**

you will need:

3 cm (1¼ in) diameter dowel:
2 x 110 cm (43 in) lengths and 2 x 64 cm (25 in) lengths

preservative wood stain

50 cm x 1.5 m (20 in x 5 ft) canvas

sewing thread

hardy hemp rope (length will vary according to where it is to be suspended)

1 Paint all the lengths of dowel with two coats of wood stain.

2 Using a 12 mm (½ in) drill bit, drill a hole 6 cm (2½ in) in from the end of each length of dowel. Fold and stitch on a sewing machine a narrow hem along the two long sides of the canvas. Then fold and stitch a hem 6 cm (2½ in) wide along both short ends of the canvas. These will form the sleeves for the dowels.

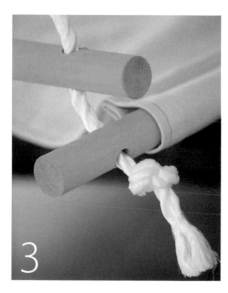

3 Thread the two shorter lengths of dowel through the canvas. Align the drilled holes of the longer and shorter dowels. Thread one end of the rope through one pair of holes at the top of the chair and tie a simple overhand knot. Thread the other end of the rope through the pair of holes at the bottom of the chair and tie a knot. Repeat with the other two dowels.

4 Hold the chair at a comfortable angle and tie a large overhand knot at the top of the ropes to form a loop to suspend it by.

Safety
Ensure the tree you choose is fit for sustained load-bearing and check the ropes regularly for wear and tear.

flowery bedroll

A pretty floral bedroll is lighter and more comfortable than a thin blanket, ideal for using around the garden or even at the beach. A generous layer of polyester wadding sandwiched between smooth, fresh cotton ensures the bedroll is a comfortable, snug resting place on almost any surface. The cover fabric could all be the same or in toning or contrasting colours. The bedroll can be waterproofed as suggested on page 55, although it is machine washable.

skill level **3**

time **2 hours**

you will need:

2 lengths cotton or poly-cotton fabric, each 4 cm (1½ in) wider and longer than the wadding

sewing thread

about 180 cm x 75 cm (6 x 2½ ft) thick polyester wadding

12 mother of pearl or pretty buttons

about 4 m (4 yd) narrow ribbon to complement the cover fabrics

1 Pin the two pieces of fabric together, right sides facing. Machine-stitch the two pieces together about 2 cm (¾ in) in from the edge, leaving about a quarter of one end open. If you wish, neaten the edges of the fabric with a zigzag stitch to stop fraying. Turn the fabric bag right side out. Lay the fabric flat on the floor and push the wadding inside. Use pins to secure the wadding at the two far corners and work down the mattress, tucking the wadding into the edges and pinning as necessary. When it is satisfactorily in place, sew up the opening by hand as neatly as possible.

2 Now add the button and ribbon decoration that holds the wadding in place. Measure 30 cm (12 in) from the top of the bedroll and 18 cm (7 in) in from one side and sew on a button, ensuring the thread goes all the way through the wadding and both layers of fabric. Then tie two short lengths of ribbon around the thread that is holding the button.

3 Measure the same distances at the other side of the bedroll and add another button and ribbon. Now add another button and ribbon every 30 cm (12 in) down from the first two, using 10 buttons in all, regularly spaced in two rows down the length of the bedroll.

4 Remove all the pins. Roll the bedroll up and sew on ribbon ties to keep it rolled. You could make a carrying handle from more ribbon held in place with the last two buttons or, as we have done here, make a fabric handle from a leftover scrap.

cushions

Garden benches, dining chairs and even a blanket on the grass are much more comfortable and inviting when heaped with plump, soft cushions. If you have the time and the sewing skills, it's a great idea to make your own cushions to fit benches and chairs and in colours to suit your garden. For extra durability you can buy weather-resistant fabric, or you can treat your own or ready-made washable cushion covers with a waterproofing solution.

ABOVE A blanket, some cushions and a sunshade can be all you need to create the most comfortable of spaces to relax.

LEFT Even the hardest of seats are rendered more welcoming with the addition of a cushion. Here the colour has been cleverly chosen to reflect the colour scheme of the garden.

BELOW Carefully chosen cushions add a splash of cheery colour as well as comfort.

Waterproofing fabric

Waterproofing solutions are generally sold for camping and hiking equipment, but are excellent for garden cushions too. Just remove the cushion pad and wash the cover in the washing machine with the recommended quantity of solution according to the manufacturer's instructions. Treating your cushion covers this way means there is no need to worry about the odd shower and damp spoiling them. Depending on how much wear your cushions get they may need reproofing annually.

bubbling bowl

The gentle sound of moving water is immensely soothing. Encrusted in a cool, reflective mosaic of ceramics and glass and filled with softly bubbling water, this bowl may help create a mood of serenity. The finished bowl can be placed on the terrace or set among a drift of low planting.

skill level 2

time 4 hours, plus drying

you will need:

large terracotta bowl, about 60 cm (2 ft) diameter

PVA glue

frostproof silicon sealant

external tile adhesive

mosaic materials: we used broken ceramic tiles, florists' glass beads, marbles and mosaic mirror tiles

external tile grout

small adjustable pond pump

1 Seal the pot inside and out with a coat of PVA glue diluted with an equal quantity of water. Seal the drainage hole with some of the silicon sealant. Drill a hole near the base of the pot for the pump cable.

2 Working over a small area at a time, spread some tile adhesive over the inside of the bowl and push the mosaic pieces into the adhesive. Continue until the whole of the inside of the pot is covered. Leave to dry.

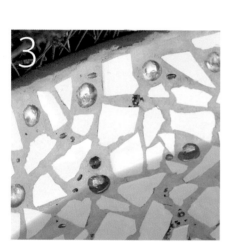

3 Use a sponge or soft cloth to force grout into the spaces between the mosaic pieces. Spread it liberally over the surface and then wipe away any excess. Ensure the cable hole doesn't get blocked. Finally, polish the mosaic clean with a soft cloth.

4 Place the pump in the bowl, thread the cable through the hole and seal it on both sides of the body of the pot with silicon sealant.

5 Hide the pump with more mosaic material and large marbles. When the sealant is dry add the water and adjust the pump. Pumps often come with many and varied fountain attachments, but settling for a small rolling plume of water usually gives the best effect.

Warning
Outdoor electrical installations should be carried out by a qualified electrician and in accordance with all safety regulations.

windbreak screen

skill level **1**

time **2 hours**

you will need:

4 m (4 yd) brightly coloured fabric

sewing thread

fabric glue (optional)

4 inexpensive curtain poles with finials (you will only need one finial per pole)

5 m (5 yd) ribbon cut into 12 equal lengths

A colourful take on the traditional windbreak, this vibrant screen can provide your own private outdoor space for a perfect afternoon of relaxation. This great summer accessory can give shelter from neighbours and chilly winds or be equally useful on the beach or on country picnics.

1 Fold over 1 cm (½ in) and then another 1 cm (½ in) of fabric all around the screen, securing it as you go with pins. (It is unnecessary to hem the selvedge.) Either sew or use fabric glue to hold the hem in place.

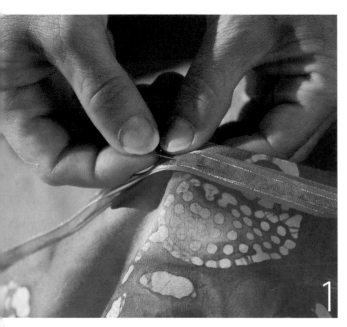

2 Spread out the fabric and position the four poles equally along its length. Mark the position for three sets of ribbon ties on each pole, at the top, bottom and middle.

3 Sew a length of ribbon at its mid-point at each of the marks.

4 To erect the screen for the first time, push the first pole firmly into the ground (if the ground is hard you may need to use a rubber mallet). Tie the end of the screen to the pole, pull the fabric taut and push in the next pole. Repeat this process with the remaining two poles.

Tip

The screen could be made longer if it is just for use in the garden. However, the more poles you include the heavier and less portable the screen becomes. As it stands it should accommodate most picnics comfortably. Don't be tempted to increase the gap between the posts by a great deal as the fabric will begin to sag.

deckchair cover

Often the canvas sling of a deckchair begins to look tatty and jaded long before the frame wears out, though this too can begin to look a little battered in time. Sprucing up a well-constructed, classic deckchair is well worthwhile; in fact, with just a little effort and not a great deal of expense an old deckchair can look far more chic and individual than one you might buy.

skill level **2**

time **3 hours**

you will need:

2 pieces fabric 3 cm (1¼ in) wider and longer than the existing sling

extra fabric for ties

sewing thread

preservative wood stain

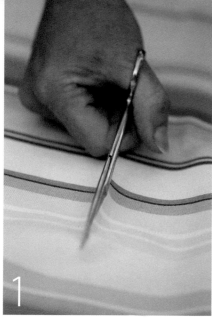

1 Cut two pieces of fabric about 3 cm longer and 3 cm (1¼ in) wider than the original sling.

2 Pin the two pieces of fabric together, right sides facing. Cut fabric for four ties, each about 50 x 5 cm (20 x 2 in). Fold each in half lengthways (right sides together) and machine-stitch across one end and along the long side. Turn right side out. Fold the four ties in half and pin them in position at the top and bottom of the sling. Tuck them in between the two layers of fabric so the folded edge is just showing.

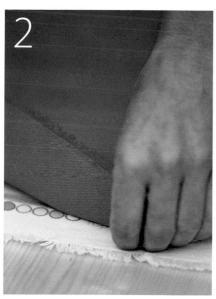

3 Sew around the pinned fabric about 1.5 cm (½ in) from the edge; leave a 20 cm (8 in) section open on one side. Ensure you sew over the ties and add an extra couple of lines of reinforcing stitching across them to hold them securely. If you wish, neaten the fabric edges with zigzag stitching. Turn the whole sling the right way out and sew up the remaining opening by hand. Lightly rub down the deckchair frame and apply two coats of preservative wood stain.

4 When the stain is dry tie the sling firmly in place.

rustic bench

This rugged, weather-worn bench, made from reclaimed timber, looks instantly at home among cottage garden or seaside planting. Reclamation yards are a good source of weathered timber, or if the smooth perfection and clean lines of new timber would suit your garden better use the same method of construction with pristine, planed wood.

skill level   **2**

time   **2 hours 30 mins, plus drying**

you will need:

2 reclaimed wooden fence posts

1 thick plank of wood, about 1.5 m (5 ft) long

2 x 12 mm (½ in) diameter dowel, as long as your plank is wide

2 bags dry cement fixing

1 With a jigsaw or handsaw cut a V-shaped notch into each end of the plank, large enough for the fence posts to sit in comfortably.

2 Put the cut plank on the ground where you want the bench and mark the position of the two posts. Dig two holes about 60 cm (2 ft) deep and just a little wider than the posts. Wedge the posts upright in the holes.

3 Use the cement mix according to the manufacturer's instructions to secure the posts in the holes. Leave to cure overnight.

4 To fit the seat, use a 12 mm (½ in) drill bit to drill a hole in each post 45 cm (18 in) from the ground. (This assumes the ground is level. If not, use a spirit level and a long piece of wood to ensure the holes are level or your seat will slope.) Push a length of dowel through each hole and lower the plank over the top of the posts until it sits on the dowel pegs.

QUICK & EASY IDEAS

RIGHT A reflective metal bowl borrowed from inside the house can be used as a temporary gazing bowl in a tranquil corner outside. Reflecting the sky and clouds, it is a feature to encourage you to pause a while and wonder at the reflections. Often ornaments and artefacts can successfully be given new life like this in the garden. Look for durable materials that will withstand prolonged rain, sun and frost or just see these features as temporary delights for the kinder months.

LEFT Choosing a tranquil planting scheme will go a long way to establishing a soothing character for your garden. Verdant gardens have a cool, relaxing ambience. Carefully stud this verdure with whites and silvers to add interest and the effect is a natural serenity. Creating enclosed areas like this one, where one feels separate from the bustle of outside world, can only reinforce this feeling.

RIGHT and FAR RIGHT A number of plants are renowned for their relaxing properties; perhaps most famed among them are lavender (far right) and chamomile (right). Use these plants in pots around the terrace, in borders or as an edging along paths so they release their soothing fragrance as you brush past.

RIGHT The musical splash of water can be a soothing addition to a garden. The water feature itself need not be elaborate; this contemporary stainless steel spout, elegantly simple, delivers a sparkling stream of water into a stainless steel cistern. An adjustable pump allows the flow and sound of the water to be finely tuned.

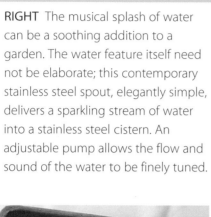

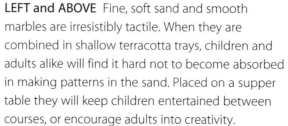

LEFT and ABOVE Fine, soft sand and smooth marbles are irresistibly tactile. When they are combined in shallow terracotta trays, children and adults alike will find it hard not to become absorbed in making patterns in the sand. Placed on a supper table they will keep children entertained between courses, or encourage adults into creativity.

decoration
and light

Decorating your garden makes it your own. Just as you decorate your home with pictures, beautiful objects and necessities that are at once useful and attractive, so you can decorate your garden. Although most of us want our garden to represent our own personal portion of the great outdoors, our own chunk of  nature, there is no reason why decorative elements cannot be used to add interest, wit and personality. The ideas in this chapter can be faithfully copied but each also presents the opportunity to take the idea further, making it your own, in the choice of pattern or colour. All the lighting projects produce a feature that is both practical and decorative, providing atmospheric lighting that can be moved around the garden.

twinkling candles

Nothing compares with the soft glow of candles for providing atmospheric lighting on a balmy summer's evening. This stylish reflective metal sconce supports seven candles, projecting their twinkling light around the garden. It is perfect for providing ambient light for al fresco dining. Made in less than two hours and weighing very little, the sconce can be hung on almost any vertical structure.

skill level **1**

time **1 hour 30 mins**

you will need:

1 sheet of mirror-finish aluminium

7 candles

7 tea light holders

3 screws

3 rawl plugs

1 Leave the protective film on the metal. Use a felt pen to mark seven strips 5 cm (2 in) wide and 10 cm (4 in) apart on to the protective film. If the base of your tea light holder is larger than 5 cm (2 in) adjust the dimensions accordingly.

2 Using tin snips cut along the lines you have marked to produce strips of random lengths, three starting from the top and three from the bottom.

3 Taking care to avoid any sharp edges, bend one of the strips up so that it is at a right angle to the metal sheet.

Why not try...

Replacing the candles with small bunches of flowers in water to provide a stunning and colourful daytime display – a charming finishing touch when you have friends around for lunch or tea in the garden.

4 Fold it twice more to form a shelf so that the remainder of the strip is in line with the original sheet. Repeat this with the remaining strips.

5 Drill three holes 1 cm (½ in) from the top edge of the sheet, one at the centre and one 2 cm (¾ in) from each edge. Finally remove the protective film.

6 Using screws and rawl plugs secure the sconce in position. Add tea light holders and candles and enjoy.

ribbon screen

Although weighted by large beads, the vibrant ribbons of this decorative yet practical screen bring movement to the garden with every breath of wind. Hang the screen from a pergola and it will obscure an ugly view or the neighbouring house; hang it across a door and it will keep insects out of the house.

skill level   1

time   2 hours

you will need:

ribbon in 3 or 4 colours

dowel, cut to the width of screen you require

2–3 cup hooks

beads – about 3–4 per strand of ribbon

jewellery-making wire

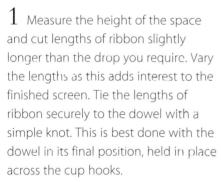

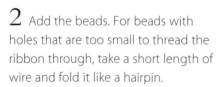

1 Measure the height of the space and cut lengths of ribbon slightly longer than the drop you require. Vary the lengths as this adds interest to the finished screen. Tie the lengths of ribbon securely to the dowel with a simple knot. This is best done with the dowel in its final position, held in place across the cup hooks.

2 Add the beads. For beads with holes that are too small to thread the ribbon through, take a short length of wire and fold it like a hairpin.

3 Push the ribbon into the folded wire and thread the two ends of the wire through the bead.

4 Twist the wire and coil it to hold the bead in position.

5 If the holes in your beads are large enough, simply thread them on to the ribbon and tie a knot just below, to stop it slipping. Attach three or four beads to each length of ribbon.

driftwood tower

Contorted, bleached and worn smooth by the sea, pieces of driftwood have a tactile, soft, organic quality, a character etched by the ocean, which never fails to appeal. These characteristics make it a perfect material for making garden features with a natural, quiet charm: beautiful, eye-catching but not overpowering.

skill level   1

time   1 hour 30 mins

you will need:

pieces of driftwood of varying lengths

1 m (3 ft) galvanized thread rod, about 8 mm ($\frac{1}{3}$ in) diameter

1 Arrange your driftwood pieces in order of size on a flat surface. Choose a large, heavy piece as the base for your tower.

2 With a drill bit to match your thread rod, make a hole at the mid-point of your chosen base piece nearly all the way through and firmly push in the thread rod.

3 Take each piece of wood in turn, starting with the longest, and drill a hole at its centre and thread it on to the rod.

4 Repeat this process until the rod is covered with all but the last piece. Drill halfway through the final piece and push it on to the top of the rod to give a neat finish.

driftwood candles

Encrusted with dripping wax and supporting flickering candles, large pieces of driftwood make an unusual centrepiece for a dining table. There is no need to stop at three candles – if your wood allows it could span the entire length of the table.

skill level 1

time 30 mins

you will need:
large piece of driftwood
3 candles

1 Try laying the driftwood on all of its sides to find a position in which it will be stable.

2 Then mark the positions for three candles and, using a 20 mm (³⁄₄ in) drill bit, make a hole about 2 cm (³⁄₄ in) deep at each point marked.

3 Push the candles firmly into position on the driftwood.

Candle power

Candlelight is as beautiful outdoors as in the house, but the same care needs to be taken. Never leave a candle unattended, and ensure all candles are set firmly in their holders and are stable, so they will not easily be knocked over. Shielding the flame in a hurricane lamp or even a simple glass jar is a good plan.

modern metal

An eye-catching focal point will enliven any garden's structure. These mirrored metal shapes make a remarkable sculpture with an ever-changing surface, reflecting everything around them. Made literally in minutes, the shapes can be easily moved around as the garden changes through the year. There is no need to stop at two triangles, a line of reflective triangles would look spectacular.

skill level **1**

time **15 mins**

you will need:

50 x 100 cm (20 x 40 in) sheet of mirror-finish aluminium

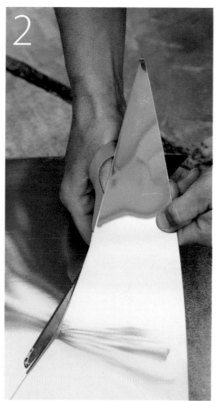

A moment's reflection

Choose the position of these reflective shapes with care – if they merge invisibly into their surroundings they could be a danger and the pointed corner or sharp edges may cause injury if someone tripped or fell on them. And of course avoid areas where children play. They are particularly effective set among planting.

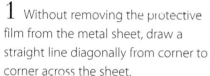

1 Without removing the protective film from the metal sheet, draw a straight line diagonally from corner to corner across the sheet.

2 Use stout scissors or tin snips to cut along the line, cutting away from you and keeping the cut as smooth and neat as possible.

3 Remove the protective film from each of the triangles.

4 Gently bend each of the triangles so it forms a gentle arc and push them into the soil so they remain upright.

outdoor picture

Climbing plants are not the only way to cheer up a drab garden wall. These bold stripes of colour combine to make a convincing artwork that will brighten the garden all year round. Perhaps most appealing is that, despite its good looks, you don't need to be an artist to create it!

skill level 1

time 3 hours

you will need:

60 x 120 cm (2 x 4 ft) marine plywood, 12 mm (½ in) thick

PVA glue

acrylic paint in four colours

extra-strong exterior double-sided tape

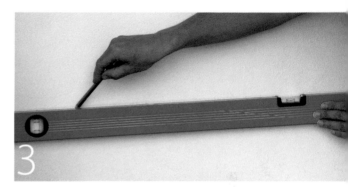

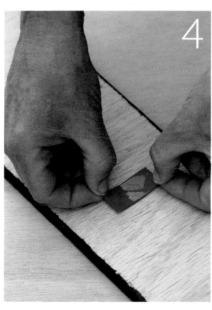

1 Cut the plywood into seven strips of different widths. Your timber supplier may do this for you. Seal both sides and the edges of each piece of timber with PVA diluted with an equal quantity of water.

2 Arrange the pieces of wood on a flat surface as you want them on the wall and carefully apply two coats of paint to each.

3 Using a spirit level, draw a straight line on the wall to mark the position of the bottom edge of the picture.

4 Attach several pieces of the double-sided tape to the back of each strip.

5 Working from one side of the picture to the other, push each strip firmly into position. Vary the gaps between the strips and ensure the bottom of each strip sits on the line and is vertical on the wall.

All the colours of the rainbow

Your combination of colours will have an impact on the look of your wall art. Try swatches of the colours together or, as acrylics often come in transparent bottles, line them up to see their effect on each other. You might choose a cool, calm mix of harmonizing blues and greys or a punchy mix of sizzling orange and zesty limes and lemons. Your selection might be based on a colour theme used in the garden, or just you own favourites.

lantern stand

Candle lanterns are a quick and inexpensive way to light the garden, where they cast a magical glitter. Often in smaller gardens and on balconies suitable supports from which to hang lanterns are difficult to find. This freestanding lantern stand solves this problem, easily supporting five lanterns anywhere you like. It can be used with bought lanterns or, as here, with pretty home-made versions.

skill level   **2**

time   **4 hours**

you will need:

5 small, attractively shaped jars

paper

repositional mount

spray glass paint

galvanized wire

2 m (6 ft) aluminium tube, 20 mm (³⁄₄ in) diameter

wooden block about 40 x 15 x 15 cm (16 x 6 x 6 in) or a natural log round

30 cm (12 in) dowel, 3 mm (¹⁄₈ in) diameter, cut into 5 equal lengths

silver paint

1 First decorate the jars. Using a coin as a template draw and cut out 35 spots from plain paper.

2 Stick seven spots on each jar, using the repositional mount. Ensure the edges are firmly stuck down.

3 Give each lantern a thin coat of glass paint.

4 When the paint is dry peel off the paper spots.

5 Make a handle for each lantern by winding wire around each jar's threaded top and looping the end from one side to the other to form a handle. Twist the ends firmly to finish.

6 Now make the stand. With a 3 mm (⅛ in) metal drill bit, drill five holes at 30 cm (12 in) intervals, measuring from one end of the aluminium tube. Drill a hole at 45 degrees in the block of wood using a 20 mm (¾ in) wood drill bit. Push the aluminium tube into the hole so it holds firm.

7 Paint the dowel pegs silver and, when they are dry, push one through each of the five holes in the tube. Hang on the lanterns.

pebble plaque

Mosaic is an amazingly durable art form ideally suited to use in the garden. Familiar as a material for decorative paving, pebble mosaic can also be used to add texture and pattern to garden walls. Here monochrome, polished river pebbles flow in an undulating design, adding a shot of texture and pattern to a rough garden wall. Rather than applying the mosaic directly to the wall it is made in a wooden tray so it can be moved around the garden.

skill level 2

time 3 hours, plus drying

you will need:

30 x 50 cm (12 x 20 in) marine plywood

PVA glue

exterior wood glue

1.65 m (5½ ft) strip wood, 32 mm (1½ in) wide

preservative wood stain

2 small eyelets

about 50 cm (20 in) galvanized wire

exterior tile adhesive

about 4 kg (9 lb) black and white river pebbles

cream exterior tile grout

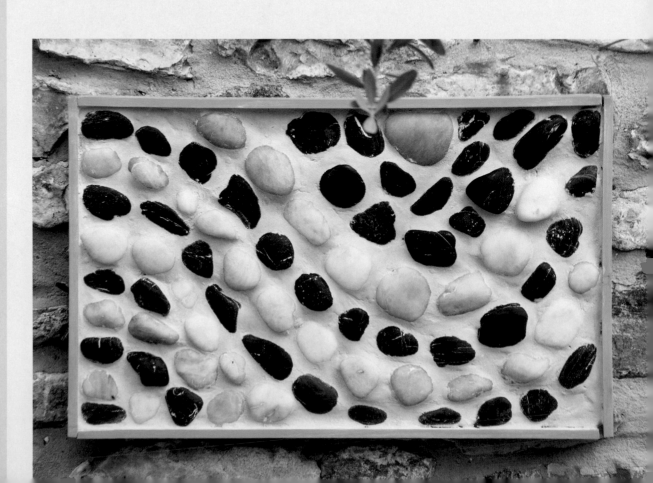

1 Seal the marine plywood with a coat of PVA diluted with an equal amount of water. Then, using the wood glue, attach the strip wood to the marine plywood base to form a tray. Leave to dry.

2 Apply two coats of wood stain to the tray and leave to dry. Screw the eyelets into the back of the frame and fasten the wire between them to hang the finished mosaic.

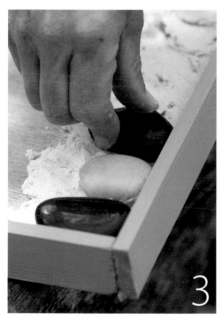

3 Draw a curving line across the base of the tray as a guide for the design. Apply the tile adhesive to a small area at a time, working across the tray and push the pebbles firmly into place. As the pebbles are fairly large and irregular be generous with the adhesive.

4 Once the adhesive has dried apply the grout. Work over the whole mosaic, using a sponge to force the grout into the gaps between the pebbles. Remove any excess.

5 Finally polish the pebbles clean with a soft cloth.

sparkling chandelier

Combining romantic, scented blooms, sparkling crystal beads and flickering candles in this planted chandelier conjures up an enchanting atmosphere when suspended above an intimate dining table.

skill level **1**

time **2 hours**

you will need:

ornamental hanging basket, 30 cm (12 in) diameter

silver spray paint

4 tea light holders

galvanized wire

basket liner

compost

3 *Nicotiana* 'Saratoga Lime'

3 white-variegated ivy

cut glass drops

crystal beads

1 Gently sand the surface of the hanging basket and remove any dust. Then apply a coat of silver paint to the basket and one side of the liner. Hanging the basket makes this much easier.

2 Once the basket is dry, wind a length of wire around each tea light holder several times, twisting the ends to hold it firmly and then use the tail ends of the wire to secure it to the basket.

3 Place the liner neatly in the basket (silver side out) and three quarters fill it with compost.

4 Remove the plants from their pots and arrange them in the basket. Firm the compost and water the basket.

5 Finally, loosely wind the length of crystal beads around the basket and its chains, and hook on the crystal drops where they will catch the light.

QUICK & EASY IDEAS

RIGHT Large glass vases make impressive storm lanterns. Use shell mulch, florists' beads, sand or pebbles to hold the candles upright and arrange them along paths to welcome your guests or set them among plants to engender an ethereal atmosphere.

BELOW Even keeping the birds happy can make the garden beautiful! This vibrant shallow glass bowl, stolen from the kitchen, makes an excellent, practical birdbath and at the same time adds a dash of bold colour among the delicate pink-tinted aquilegias.

RIGHT Pumpkin and squash lanterns don't have to be saved for Halloween. Cut geometric shapes instead of ghoulish faces to make appealing lanterns to light up any occasion.

ABOVE Small decorative touches can make a garden special. These pastel crystals shimmer in the sun, casting dancing spots of light around them – a superb way to dress the garden for a special lunch or party, or pep up a tree after it has bloomed.

ABOVE Mirrors make fantastic adornments for dark corners of the garden, reflecting light around the garden. A bright frame defines the mirror, announcing its presence, but remove the frame and nestle the mirror among foliage to extend the garden and you can create deceptive vistas into parts of a secret garden that don't actually exist.

TOP RIGHT Light shines through these glass vases, creating fantastic effects in the garden beyond as flashes of blue light dart across it.

ABOVE With colours deftly chosen to sit well on the painted trellis, this large piece of abstract art brings life to a compact dining area. The bold effect is easily replicated with acrylic paints on marine plywood.

LEFT Simply arranging a trio of spotlights in a swathe of grasses creates a dramatic lighting effect: a brilliantly atmospheric light show.

QUICK & EASY IDEAS

LEFT Made distinguished and handsome by years of service in the garden, these utilitarian watering cans line up to become an apt and charming garden feature. Many everyday and unlikely objects can gain similar impact collected and displayed in groups like this.

RIGHT A smart, decorative edging to define areas of planting and paths gives the garden a crisp definition, makes the garden look tidy and reinforces its structure. Constructing an edging need not be a massive undertaking; these edgings work well, each in its own way and each is simply placed in position.

FAR RIGHT The ends of canes used to support planting can be hard to see and have the potential to cause eye injuries. Slipping a colourful glass bottle over the end not only makes them visible but makes a virtue out of a necessity.

LEFT The rugged rocks have an untamed, natural appearance, contrasting with yet suiting the loose, fluid planting they strive to contain. In contrast, the overlapping flat slabs of natural stone have much neater character. The bleached shells are pure fun – a great finishing touch for a seaside garden.

FAR LEFT and LEFT Paths are essential to get around the garden but this does not mean they have to be plain. Crushed shells make a crunchy path with an interesting texture that should also inhibit the movement of slugs and snails around the garden. Log rounds set with the end grain uppermost make a path with a hardwearing surface as well as an interesting pattern.

ABOVE Slung with seemingly little artifice around a post, these shells and floats are a simple but very successful outdoor decoration.

ABOVE and RIGHT Each piece one of a kind, these weather-worn pieces of wood merely thrust into the ground at the back of an area of wild planting give a diaphanous planting a rhythm that pleases the eye.

stylish ways
with plants

Leaves and flowers, the greenery of nature, are, ultimately, what define a garden – only the most avant garde or perhaps most neglected of gardens are completely without plants. Most of us want to be surrounded by appealing planting in our gardens but few of us have the time to devote hours to their cultivation.

The trick is to use planting schemes and methods of cultivation that require little effort once planted, yet look fantastic. Whether you long for the appeal of the well-orchestrated, traditional border, the informality of wild flowers or require just a few chic containers for a patio garden this chapter offers some interesting and unusual solutions.

architectural aquatics

Striking aquatic plants make unusual and sophisticated container subjects when housed in large glass vases. The elegant architectural form of papyrus (*Cyperus papyrus*) makes it an obvious choice, although other aquatic plants would work just as well.

you will need:
3 large glass vases
pebbles
3 papyrus or other
architectural aquatic plants

1 Half fill each vase with water and put a layer of pebbles 5–7 cm (2–3 in) deep at the bottom.

2 Gently lower the papyrus into position, trying not to agitate the soil (do not remove the plant from the pot). Holding the plant upright, pack pebbles around the pot so it is completely hidden.

3 Add a layer of pebbles on the surface of the pot and slowly top up the vase with water.

vertical veg

Nothing tastes quite so good as home-grown fruit and vegetables eaten fresh from the plant, but sadly few of us have the time, space or inclination to tend a full-scale kitchen garden. An alternative is to grow just a few choice plants in a large container; the harvests may not be enormous but large enough to make the effort, which is minimal, well worthwhile. A large container with planting holes in its body makes the most of the space and provides plenty of growing room for the plants.

skill level **2**

time **2 hours 30 mins**

you will need:

galvanized dustbin

drainage material:
crocks or gravel

compost

vegetable and herb plants
(see box on page107)

1 Make several drainage holes in the bottom of the dustbin, using a hammer and nail or a drill.

2 To make the planting holes, mark five circles randomly spaced on the front of the dustbin. A mug or plastic cup is a useful size to draw around.

3 Cut out the holes by drilling a hole just inside the margin of the marked circle, large enough to insert the blade of a jigsaw. Use the jigsaw to cut out the disc of metal. Take care of the sharp edges.

4 The container is best planted up in situ, as once filled with compost it is very heavy. Put a layer of gravel or broken crocks in the bottom of the dustbin and fill it with compost up to the first planting hole.

5 Remove a plant from its pot and push the rootball through the hole. Firm the compost around the rootball and add another layer of compost up to the next planting pocket. Continue this process until the whole bin is full. Add more plants in the top of the container. If you are using small plants place a piece of black polythene inside the planting hole and cut a slit in this to plant through.

maintenance

Most plants will appreciate a sunny location and require the compost to be kept moist. After a few weeks the nutrients in the compost will be depleted so begin feeding with an all-purpose plant food in accordance with the manufacturer's instructions. Including a slow-release fertilizer in the compost when you plant the dustbin will cut down on maintenance.

herbs and vegetables

A myriad of different plants will thrive in the planter. We grew two varieties of tomato ('Tumbling Tom Yellow' and 'Totem', a bush type), a chilli called 'Apache', patio sweet peppers, strawberry 'Elsanta', oregano, coriander and purple basil. Strawberries and sun-loving herbs like thyme and basil are especially suited to growing in the planting holes. Any patio varieties of pepper, aubergines, chilli and squashes will do well, as will courgettes, although their large leaves may swamp other plants. Regular vine tomatoes should flourish in the top of the container with the addition of a stake; just remember to pinch out the side shoots. Cut and come again salad leaves are a good use of space and quickly grow from seed.

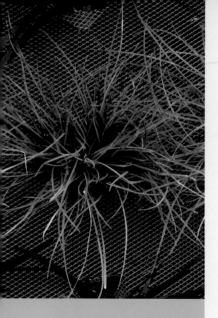

plant picture

Two plants with amazing textures and colours have been used in this vertical planter to create a living picture to add an element of surprise to any garden wall or fence. Both plants are evergreen and will require little care beyond watering, for which the picture must be removed briefly from the wall.

skill level 1

time 2 hours

you will need:

wire

50 x 30 cm (20 x 12 in) planting tray

6 *Ophiopogon planiscapus nigrescens*

6 *Festuca glauca* 'Elijah Blue'

compost

50 x 30 cm (20 x 12 in) weed-proof membrane

sheet of galvanized mesh a little larger than the tray

1 Thread a length of wire through two of the drainage holes in the tray and wind the ends together to form a loop to hang the picture.

2 Remove the plants from their pots and space them equally in the tray in four alternating stripes each with three plants. Pack compost firmly around the plants' rootballs.

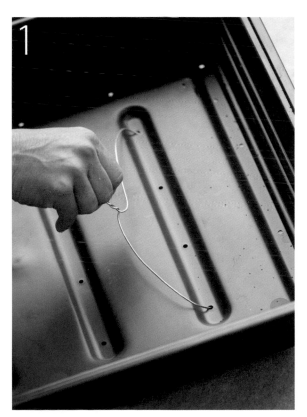

3 Cut the membrane to fit the top of the tray, then cut cross-shaped slots to feed each of the plants through. Fit the membrane neatly round the base of the plants and tuck it down into the compost. Repeat the process with the galvanized mesh, tucking the wire ends down around the plants. Pierce holes in the rim of the tray and thread short lengths of wire through the holes and the mesh, twisting them to hold the mesh securely. Fold the edges of the metal sheet around the tray. The picture will benefit from a couple of weeks standing horizontal to allow the plants to root into the compost before being hung on the wall.

thyme heart

Fragrant, floriferous and amazingly resilient, thyme makes the perfect subject for this unusual planting method. This romantic, pretty herb heart can be suspended from a tree or pergola or just planted on one side and used to perk up a lacklustre wall. To keep the heart looking smart and neat, trim the thyme after its flowers fade.

skill level 1

time 2 hours

you will need:

large sheet of paper

30 x 80 cm (12 x 32 in) square-holed, galvanized metal mesh

30 x 80 cm (12 x 32 in) hessian (burlap)

compost

25 thyme plugs or plantlets

short length of wire

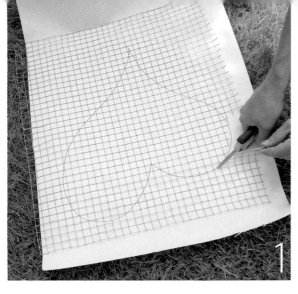

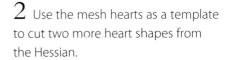

1 Draw a heart shape on a piece of paper, making it about 30 cm (12 in) wide and 40 cm (16 in) long. Use this as a guide to cut two heart shapes from the metal mesh. Take care with any sharp ends of the wire.

2 Use the mesh hearts as a template to cut two more heart shapes from the Hessian.

3 Sandwich the two pieces of hessian between the two mesh shapes and fold over the edges so the four layers are held together securely, leaving about a 10 cm (4 in) opening on one side.

4 Fill the heart with compost through the opening so it is firm and expands into a gently bowed, cushion shape. Now fold over the wire and hessian of the opening to seal.

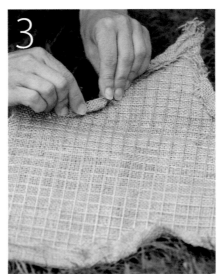

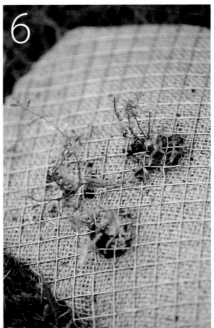

5 Cut a small cross shape in the mesh using wire cutters, folding back the edges. Cut through the hessian below in a similar way, using scissors.

6 Carefully ease a little plant into the compost and fold back the hessian and mesh to hold it in position. Repeat this process with all 25 plants, spacing them evenly over the heart. Water well but carefully. Make a hook or loop from a length of wire and hang up in position. The small plants will spread to cover the entire surface of the heart.

perennial lawn

Even a patch of uninspiring lawn takes a surprising amount of time to maintain. However, stud the lawn with perennial plants and there is no maintenance to be done from spring to autumn and the flat green grass is replaced by a billowing mass of meadow-like planting. Grass seedheads and the blooms of the perennials create a fluid, ever-changing picture as the season progresses.

skill level **2**

time **variable according to area**

you will need:

3–4 perennial plants in 9 cm (3½ in) pots per square metre or yard of lawn

We used scabious (*Scabiosa caucasica*) and a golden variety of achillea (*A. filipendulina*), but you could try globe thistle (*Echinops*), *Knautia* 'Melton Pastels', cone flowers (*Echinacea*) or the daisy-like *Boltonia asteroides*.

1 Lay out all the plants over the area you intend to plant. Keep the spacing between plants and the mix of plants random but aim for an overall density of about three or four plants per square metre/yard.

2 To plant the perennials, cut out a small square of turf and dig a hole slightly larger than the pot. Remove the plant from its pot, gently lower it into the hole and firm the soil back around the plant.

maintenance

In the early autumn, cut the whole area, first using a strimmer and then with a lawnmower. The grass should regenerate quickly and look like a normal lawn all winter, only to burst into flower next summer. Alternatively the seedheads can be left to stand, golden and parched, all winter. Drenched with soft autumn light and later dusted with snow and sparkling frost, the plants have a whole new look.

mobile fruit screen

Easily moved around the terrace on its hidden wheels, this stylish and practical wooden planter with a built-in contemporary trellis can provide shade, create shelter from the wind or act as a screen to obscure an ugly view or the view of others wherever needed. This planter contains an ancient vine and strawberry plants but could just as easily hold a floriferous climbing plant and colourful annuals.

skill level **3**

time **8 hours**

you will need:

6.8 m (22 ft) planking,
25 x 265 mm (1 x 10 in)

5.5 m (18 ft) batten,
32 mm (1½ in) square

3.8 mm (³⁄₁₆ in) screws

120 cm x 50 cm (48 x 20 in)
marine plywood

2 x 1.9 m (6 ft) battens,
25 x 50 mm (1 x 2 in)

about 14 lengths of
1.2 m (4 ft) batten,
32 x 12 mm (1½ x ½ in)
(see step 8)

20 mm (³⁄₄ in) screws

4 wheels

preservative wood stain

butyl or polythene liner

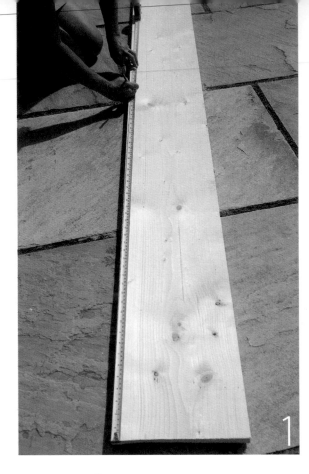

1 Measure and cut the 28 x 265 mm (1 x 10 in) planking into four 1.2 m (4 ft) lengths and four 50 cm (20 in) lengths. These will form the sides of the box.

2 Using a 6 mm (¼ in) drill bit, drill and countersink three holes equally spaced at the ends of each length of timber. In the four short lengths, position the holes 2 cm (¾ in) in from the edge, and for the others, position them 4 cm (1½ in) in.

3 Use a handsaw to cut four 52 cm (21 in) lengths of 32 mm (1½ in) batten. These are the corner battens.

4 Now make one end of the planter box. Using 3.8 mm (³⁄₁₆ in) screws through the pre-drilled holes, screw two of the 50 cm (20 in) planks to one of the corner battens. Ensure the batten ends are flush with the top and side edges of the planks. Screw down the other ends to a second batten. Repeat to make the other end of the mobile planter.

5 Stand the two ends on their sides and screw on two of the 1.2 m (4 ft) planks to form the front. Ensure the edges are flush. Turn the structure over and repeat to make the back.

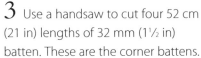

6

6 Place the shell of the planter on the sheet of plywood and draw around the inside. Use a jigsaw or handsaw to cut out the marked out shape of the base. Drill eight 25 mm (1 in) holes in the base for drainage. Measure the depth of your wheels (including fittings) and mark with pencil all around the inside bottom of the planter shell 1 cm ($^1/_2$ in) less than your wheel measurement. Screw 32 mm ($1^1/_2$ in) batten around the inside of the shell with its lower edge against the pencil rule. Drop the base into position onto the batten and screw down. Turn the planter upside down and screw on the wheels.

7 Now make the trellis. Using 3.8 mm ($^3/_{16}$ in) screws, attach the two 1.9 m (6 ft) lengths of batten to the inside of the back of the planter, at points 40 cm and 80 cm (16 and 32 in) along its inside length. Check they stand vertically. Cut a piece of wood 10 cm (4 in) long as a guide and, using 20 mm ($^3/_4$ in) screws, attach the 1.2 m (4 ft) lengths of batten to the vertical struts, 10 cm (4 in) apart. Add extra horizontals to make groups of five, three and three or however you wish. Apply two coats of wood stain to the whole structure. When it is dry line the planter with thick polythene or butyl liner punctured in the base and your screen is ready for planting.

7

planting plans to copy

Planting a border from scratch can be a daunting task – combining plants successfully to achieve the effect you want and a 'designed look' is never easy, especially with limited plant knowledge. The essence of most successful planting is keeping things simple, so these planting plans to copy do just that. They each have their own striking personality and each design can be repeated as many times as is required to fill your border, giving rhythm, structure and a sophisticated look to the overall scheme. If your space is wider than the example then merely add more plants to each grouping, extending the depth of border they cover.

pretty blues and yellows

This planting uses grasses and perennials for a pretty, fluid and natural look. The scheme develops through the summer and reaches its peak in late summer. The grasses and seedheads should stand through the winter and provide another dazzling display in the frost. To get the show off to an early start you could add spring bulbs to the display around the grasses, particularly the stipas, as these will make an early show. Reliable spring bulbs for this scheme include: *Narcissus* 'Yellow Cheerfulness', *Tulipa* 'Montecarlo', *Muscari latifolium* and *Crocus* 'Gypsy Girl'.

Planting list:

For each 2.5 m (8 ft) length of border 2 m (6 ft) deep

5 *Viola cornuta* (D)

3 *Campanula glomerata* 'Superba' (G)

5 *Eragrostis curvata* 'Totnes Burgundy' (H)

2 *Stipa tenuissima* 'Pony Tails' (B)

5 *Echinacea purpurea* 'Alba' (C)

1 *Hemerocallis* 'Happy Returns' (F)

5 *Salvia* (C)– choose from a wide range of perennial species

5 *Festuca glauca* 'Elijah Blue' (E)

3 *Achillea* 'Inca Gold' (A)

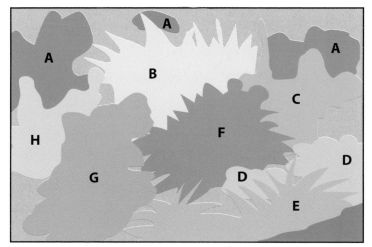

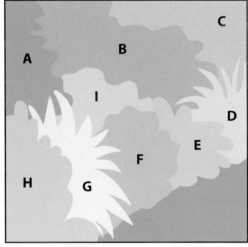

Planting list:

For each 2.5 m (8 ft) length
of border 2 m (6 ft) deep
Potentilla (H)
6 *Papaver* 'Ladybird' (F)
3 *Lobelia* 'Queen
Victoria'(G)
3 *Carex* 'Bowles Golden' (D)
3 *Dahlia* 'Bishop of
Llandaff' (I)
7 *Crocosmia* 'Lucifer' (B)
3 *Macleaya Cordata* (C)
3 *Corylus Purpurea*
'Maxima' (A)
3 *Rheum Palmatum* 'Ace
of Hearts' (E)

red-hot reds

Ablaze with vibrant reds, this border is bold and brilliant, and repeating it along a sweep of border will increase its power. Once established, the fabulous planting will smoulder on through the summer and the seedheads of the crocosmia and poppy will continue to provide structure and form until they are cut back in late winter. For reliable spring colour add the voluptuous, red parrot tulip 'Rococo' and the rich ruby tulip 'Red Wing' among the planting at the front of the border. Here the planting is set against a backdrop of *Corylus purpurea* 'Maxima' and *Macleaya cordata*, but it will work well against any dark green hedge or verdant backdrop. If you plan to plant against a bare fence, hide it with rampant climbers.

Planting list:

For each 2 m (6 ft) length of border 1.5 m (5 ft) deep

2 *Buxus sempervirens* spheres (I)
10 *Galium odorata* (H)
3 *Lamium* 'White Nancy' (G)
1 *Matteuccia struthiopteris* (E)
2 *Hosta* 'Francis Williams' (J)
3 *Dicentra spectabilis* 'Alba' (D)
1 *Myrrhis odorata* (B)
1 *Crambe cordifolia* (C)
10 *Tulipa* 'Spring Greens' (L)
30 *Tulipa* 'White Triumphator' (A)
3 *Pulmonaria* 'Sissinghurst White' (F)
3 *Narcissus Geranium* (K)

shady spring white and green

This spring planting scheme cleverly uses white to lift the gloom, using plants suited to a shady location. Gleaming out among the verdant foliage the white blooms are not the only interest, as the varied forms of foliage and growth give the planting interesting texture. The repetition of formal clipped box spheres nestling among less structured plants forms the mainstay of the scheme, present throughout the year. Other foliage plants will keep their appeal through the seasons, but for summer flowers add one of the many shade-loving perennial geraniums and spires of white foxglove (*Digitalis purpurea* 'Alba') to the frothing flowers of the crambe.

wild flower beds

you will need:

wild flower plants, as plugs
or in 9 cm (3½ in) pots

Usually a density of five or
six plants per square metre
or yard is sufficient, but
your supplier should
advise you on the density
required for the species
you select

Corralled in a curved bed in an area of lawn, wild flowers make a spirited and remarkable display. Choose plants native to your area and soil type and they will grow, perhaps unsurprisingly, like weeds, needing no care beyond a little watering while they establish. Beyond the robustness of the plants and the beauty of their blooms, one of the joys of this style of planting is that there are no weeds. Any plant that arrives can legitimately be seen as a serendipitous addition to the scheme, unless you dislike it! This is gardening for the slightly rebellious or the gardener who welcomes blooms from spring to autumn in return for just a bout of strimming a couple of times a year, and not for the really tidy gardener. The burgeoning beds will attract insect and bird life. The plants will set seed and new plants will grow, inevitably from year to year growing conditions will favour a particular species and the balance of plants in the beds will change. In all but extreme cases this will be a process of ebb and flow and require no intervention; in fact, these yearly changes and mutability are part of the appeal of any naturalized planting scheme.

1   Mark out your bed with a length of hose or rope. This gives plenty of opportunity to get the shape right.

2 Using a turf cutter, remove the grass from this area, together with a slice of the topsoil. Wild flowers usually thrive in poor soils. The fertilized soil of a lawn will not suit them as much as the impoverished soil beneath.

3 Place the plants in groups of five or seven randomly over the area you have cleared. If the area is only viewed from one side, place the taller plants towards the back with a few taller surprises at the front, but generally an undulating mishmash of heights produces the best effect.

4 When you are happy with the arrangement remove the plants from their pots and plant them in the place where they stood.

QUICK & EASY IDEAS

LEFT A small scrap of fabric and a length of raffia can really transform a potted plant straight from the garden centre into something special. Roll the pot in a length of fabric, tuck the ends in underneath and tie raffia or ribbon around its girth.

BELOW LEFT Swathed in fabric chosen to show off its colouring a simple plant becomes a pretty table centrepiece, or window ledge or doorstep decoration. It is also a great way to gift-wrap plants.

BELOW Almost anything that will hold potting compost and allow water to drain away can be used as a container. Baskets lined with perforated plastic are perfect for holding pretty, romantic arrangements of plants. Here scented hyacinths, pale yellow pansies and trailing ivy make a fresh, simple, spring display.

LEFT If space is limited, using wall-mounted containers will increase your options. Herbs make particularly good subjects for wall planters, their fresh green foliage looks great and they are on hand to add zest and flavour to barbecue cooking.

ABOVE and LEFT The constant need to water container plants can be a nuisance; one solution is to grow succulents such as aeoniums, echivera and houseleeks in containers. Adapted to life in arid conditions, they will survive happily with minimal watering.

QUICK & EASY IDEAS

LEFT and BOTTOM LEFT The growing habit of tumbling cherry tomatoes and strawberries mean they can be grown successfully in a hanging basket. With regular watering and feeding just one basket can provide a prodigious crop and provide a cascade of colour.

BELOW Used with confidence and panache, even an uninspiring tin can becomes an attractive wall planter. Recycled objects, looked at with an imaginative eye, often make interesting containers or cache-pots.

ABOVE Thoughtfully painted to complement the surrounding planting, these sturdy wooden labels are easy to make from lengths of timber battening.

TOP RIGHT Shallow bowls and containers crammed with bulbs are an easy way to ensure you have seasonal colour in the garden. Planted in the autumn, they need little care through the winter. If you miss the opportunity to plant your own bulbs, cheat – buy pots of bulbs from garden centres just before they are about to flower, remove them from their pots and cram them into your own.

RIGHT Double your plant impact by the clever use of mirror tiles. Placed on a gravel surface they reflect the planting and create interesting, shifting images.

ABOVE Plant labels don't have to be small, ugly and plastic, they can actually add to the good looks of the garden. Larger labels are less likely to get lost among the planting and easier to read. These vivid blue bottles with white lettering are hard to miss and look stunning when they are backlit.

play

Playing outdoors is an important part of a child's development, here they learn to use their skills, imagination and daring away from the restrictions necessarily imposed inside the house. So some provision for fun and playfulness is a vital part of any family garden, and not just for the children. When children use the garden to  play, beyond providing special play features the whole garden should be looked at with their safety in mind. If children are to play unsupervised the garden must be safe and free from obvious hazards like ponds and the less obvious, casually discarded sharp tools, garden chemicals and highly toxic plants. Making the garden safe, but not without challenges, gives both you and your children more freedom to relax and enjoy yourselves.

flower button swings

Utterly charming, these pretty little flowers make practical swings for children age 3 and above, and provide a splash of irresistible colour in the garden all year round. Once the flower shapes are cut out and sanded older children can even paint their own exotic bloom.

skill level **2**

time **2 hours, plus drying**

you will need:

12 mm (½ in) thick marine or exterior plywood – each swing will need about 40–45 cm (16–18 in) square

acrylic paint

hardy hemp rope

1 Draw a simple flower shape on to the plywood. Aim to make it about 40 cm (16 in) across at its widest point. Quirky flowers drawn freehand work well but if you are concerned about getting the shape right make a card stencil to draw around.

2 Cut around the shape you have drawn with a jigsaw and thoroughly sand the edges to remove any splinters and blunt the edges.

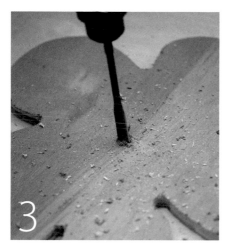

3 Using a 10 mm (³⁄₈ in) drill bit, make a hole at the centre of the flower and once again sand thoroughly.

4 Give your flower two coats of paint and leave it to dry.

5 Tie an overhand knot at one end of the length of rope and thread the other through the flower until it sits on the knot.

6 Finally tie the swing in position. Calculate the height carefully so children can easily get on and off the swing; this will probably be lower than you at first imagine. Select a robust support and regularly check all parts of the swing for wear and tear.

hanging cocoon

What child could resist the novelty of this cosy, suspended hideaway that is constantly moving and yet inside feels safe and secure. The cocoon should not be too far off the ground, just at the height that the children can steady it and climb in and out safely. You could also provide a step and anchor the base of the cocoon to the ground.

skill level **2**

time **4 hours**

you will need:

120 cm (4 ft) square marine plywood, 12 mm ($^1/_2$ in) thick

at least 12 m (40 ft), 8 mm ($^1/_3$ in) diameter hardy hemp rope (the exact length required will depend on where you suspend your cocoon)

2 m (6$^1/_2$ ft) x 178 cm (71 in) tent canvas

sewing thread

23 x 15 mm ($^5/_8$ in) eyelets

about 6 m (20 ft) strong nylon cord

1 Tie a pen to a piece of string, measure out 60 cm (2 ft) of string and pin to the centre of the board. Keeping the string taut, draw a circle. Mark five equally spaced points around the edge of the circle and drill a hole with a 10 mm (³⁄₈ in) drill bit at each point about 2 cm (³⁄₄ in) in from the edge. Cut out the circle you have drawn using a jigsaw.

2 Cut five equal lengths of rope 2.5 m (8 ft) or so long and thread one through each of the holes, securing it with an overhand knot underneath the plywood disc. With the disc on the ground hold all the ropes together about 1.3 m (4 ft) above its centre and tie all of them together with a large overhand knot. Use the remaining rope to tie it in position. Ensure the support you choose is robust enough to support sustained load-bearing.

3 Lay the canvas out on a large flat surface. Mark a point 132 cm (52 in) along one of the longer sides and then a point 66 cm (26 in) along the opposite side, measuring each from the same end. Draw a line joining your two points to each other and two other lines joining the points to the corners of the canvas, to form four interlocking triangles (the ones at either end will be right-angled triangles half the width of the two big triangles). Cut out the triangles. Machine-stitch the two largest triangles together by one of their longer sides, then stitch one of the smaller triangles

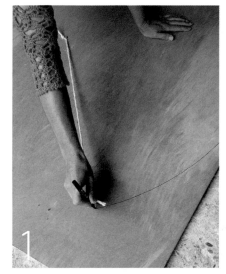

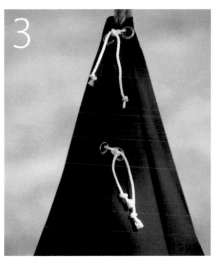

on either end. Add eyelets all along the edges, spacing them about 20–30 cm (8–12 in) apart. Where there is no selvedge fold over the edge of the fabric before riveting. Wrap the tent around the hanging platform and thread nylon cord through the topmost eyelets to secure above the knot.

4 Thread a length of strong nylon cord through the rivet holes around the base of the cocoon platform and pull it tight underneath the platform, tying it securely. The front edges are left open to form the door but can be tied together for more privacy.

tree platforms and houses

skill level **3**

time **variable depending on size**

You will need

timber (see cutting list on page 139)

small amount of hardcore

concrete

coach bolts and thread rod and bolts

screws

gate and hinges (if using)

ladder (fixed, rope or scramble net)

preservative wood stain

The superlative garden den for both children and adults is the tree house. As varied in form as the trees that support them, tree houses come in many guises, from a small temporary platform lashed to stout branches and populated by adventurous children to a sophisticated, comfortable adult retreat with wood-burning stove and television. Arguably, the appeal of tree houses are that they are unlike any other structure – held aloft and set apart from surrounding normality, yet affording a wonderful bird's-eye view of what is going on below. And the constant whisper of the breeze among the foliage endows the tree house with either an ambience of peace and tranquillity or of secrecy and adventure, depending on its style and occupants. It is neither a quick nor inexpensive project, but definitely one worth the investment. The steps here are for general guidance; the exact dimensions of your platform will by necessity be dictated by your site, your tree and your needs.

Building a tree house

You don't have to be the owner of a magnificent, aged tree to construct a tree house – a self-supporting structure can be built on legs around a small tree, giving the semblance and feel of a tree house. However, you will need a tree of some sort, plus competent carpentry and DIY skills. Sometimes a combination of construction techniques are required: some bracing to the tree and some support from legs or stilts; the exact configuration has to be judged according to the form of the tree. This versatile tree platform is perhaps the simplest construction possible, as it does not rely on its host tree for any support. Built at this height, older children could use it as a place to play; built at a lower level it will appeal to younger children or, equipped appropriately, it becomes a magical raised terrace for adults. The ambience will depend on how it is furnished. The platform can support a number of 'extras': hammocks, swings, slides, scramble nets, baskets on pulleys for supplies and telescopes. Canvas canopies or camouflage netting could be slung from the tree trunk to create a shady roof or twinkling fairy lights strewn along the handrail for a romantic gathering. Robustly constructed, the tree house also works as a base for further construction, perhaps an open-fronted shelter or a small playhouse.

Planning tips

– Always get the health of the tree checked by a qualified arborist before you begin any work. Explain your plans to the tree expert and seek advice.
– Check local planning regulations as these may impose restrictions covering tree houses.
– Plan your own safety while working in the tree. Ladders may be adequate but if you plan to build high up you may need to use ropes and safety harnesses; it may be necessary to wear a hard hat. Consider using pulleys or a block and tackle to hoist equipment into the tree.
– Think carefully about the location, the tree and the people who will use it before deciding on the height and dimensions of the platform.

Calculating timber cutting list:

All timber should be pressure-treated softwood

Legs: 150 x150 mm (6 x 6 in)
– To the planned height of the platform above ground level, add 70 cm (28 in) to be set into the ground and 1.1 m (3½ ft) to support the balustrade. Add a further 1 m (3 ft) or more if you decide to extend the legs up to support canopies or a future roof.

Joists: 200 x 50 mm (8 x 2 in)
– The length of each joist length is the same as the proposed length of your platform. You will need enough to be spaced every 60 cm (2 ft) across the platform's width and two further lengths as long as your platform as wide plus 10 cm (4 in). (These are called bearers in the steps on pages 140–141.)

Posts: 100 x100 mm (4 x 4 in) timber
– These form the main uprights in the balustrading around the platform. You will need enough 1.1 m (3½ ft) lengths to be spaced at about 1 m (1 yd) intervals around the perimeter of the platform.

Balustrades: 100 x 25 mm (4 x 1 in)
– These fill in between the posts. You will need enough 1 m (1 yd) lengths to go around the entire perimeter of the platform, allowing 10 cm (4 in) spaces for each post.

Rails: 100 x 50 mm (4 x 2 in)
– Enough for two rails along each side of the platform.
– Decking boards, planed on at least one side, sufficient to cover the surface of your platform with a 5 cm (2 in) overhang all around if desired. Having a single board run the entire breadth of the platform always looks elegant if the size allows.

1 Soak the ends of the legs in wood preservative overnight. Dig four holes at least 75 cm (2½ ft) deep, compact a small amount of hardcore in the base and set a post in each hole. Brace them to hold them exactly vertical and pour in the concrete. Leave this to cure overnight.

2 To construct the horizontal support for the platform, first build a frame around the legs with four joist lengths. Measure up the legs to the proposed platform height, then deduct the thickness of your decking. This will mark the height of the upper side of the joists. Attach the two side supports first, extending 5 cm (2 in) beyond the legs at the back – to the front the joists will extend further, to create a balcony. Check they are level and use coach bolts to secure them in position.

3 Complete the framework at the front and back with the bearers (see timber list). Position them under the first two joists, check they are level and bolt them to the legs. Now bolt the joists, running front to back, on to the bearers, working around the tree trunk, leaving no more than 60 cm (2 ft) between joists.

4 Starting at one end, nail the decking boards to the joists, leaving a 1 cm ($\frac{1}{2}$ in) gap between the boards (this will allow rain to escape) and creating a 5 cm (2 in) overhang all round. Leave reasonable room for movement around the trunk.

5 Bolt four rail lengths around the legs 20 cm (8 in) above the surface of the platform and another four lengths 1 m (1 yd) above the platform.

6 Screw the balustrades to the inside of this framework at 10 cm (4 in) intervals, adding a post after every nine balustrades. (You will have to adjust this according to the measurements of your platform.) For the entrance leave out two or three balustrades to create a 40–60 cm ($1\frac{1}{2}$–2 ft) gap where you want the ladder positioned (children will clamber over or under the rails across the gap.) Fit a gate if preferred.

7 Apply a preservative wood stain to the entire structure. Although using pressure-treated wood, the addition of wood stain will help the wood resist decay and improve its colour.

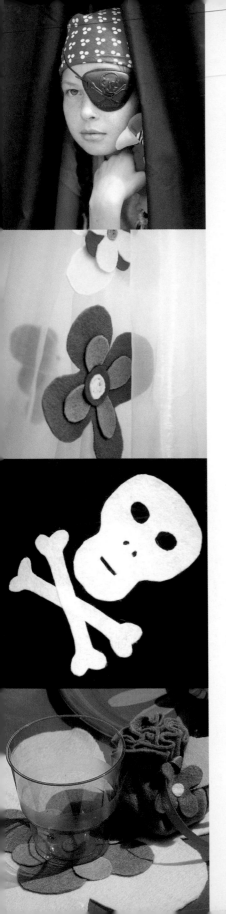

pirates and princesses party

There doesn't have to be a special occasion to have a party – organizing an imaginative party in the garden can provide children with a couple of days of fun as well as the pleasure of spending time with friends at a great party at the end of all the planning and preparations. Planning a party is a great diversion for the long summer holidays; children themselves will often have fantastic ideas and enjoy putting them into practice. These suggestions for a princess and pirates party should offer something for everyone, with plenty of opportunities to dress up, decorate the garden and invent suitable games. All without having to worry about creating a mess in the house!

pirate den

The pirate's version of the turret, made of suitably black cotton sheeting and flying the Jolly Roger, is far more mysterious and menacing, but made in just the same way.

princess turret

Just big enough for a princess and a close friend, these shimmering flower-strewn hideaways are a good way to get the party started and everyone settled. Each princess can decorate her own turret with felt flowers glued into position. The turrets are simply a length of inexpensive voile tacked on to a hula-hoop, gathered at the top and secured with a ribbon. They can either be held aloft with a central pole pushed into the ground or suspended from a tree, a washing line or a temporary string set up for the occasion.

treasure hunt

You can make a complex treasure hunt with clues hidden around the garden, one leading to the next, or stick to a simple pictorial map to follow, depending on the age of your guests. Whichever you choose, keep things authentic – age the paper in the oven or with cold coffee to make it look like an ancient relic and remember: X always marks the spot. If circumstances allow, burying the treasure is always a hit, even if it is only in the sand pit, but remember to have small spades to hand. Edible treasures are best hidden above ground.

dressing up

Making your costume can be part of the party fun. Simple props, card and lengths of irresistible fabric can transform your guests for the duration of the party, though older siblings and parents may be called upon to help.

the magic tree

Pure fun, making a magic tree gives a dead branch new life and provides a novel and enticing centrepiece for the party. It can be used as a prop in imaginative party games, danced around or just used for decoration. Spray your branch a vibrant pink, 'plant' it in a shimmering silver pot and hang it with bejewelled delights such as lollipops.

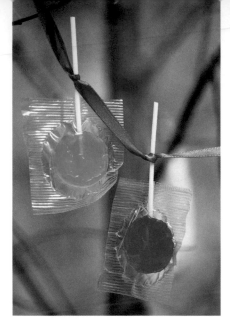

the feast

Every party needs a feast, and with young children that feast can be far simpler if served on a bright cloth on the terrace or lawn – no chairs to wobble on, or fall from and no problem if you need to change places to sit with a friend. Decorative napkin rings and placemats are fun for children to make.

pirate boats

Constructing pirate boats is a great craft activity to get children settled. For most ages it is best to have the blank boats ready and leave them to add names and decoration. Take a square cardboard box and cut out the top and bottom. Staple elastic braces to the box, taping over any sharp ends on the staples. Provide each pirate with two galleon shapes cut out of stout paper or card and let them decorate their own boat. Once finished, staple the two galleons around the box and the pirates are ready to weigh anchor and set sail on their treasure hunt.

pirate presents

Young Blackbeards will love going home with sweets in an appropriately piratical wrapping. Cut a circle of black felt with a jagged edge, place some sweets at the centre, tie the top with twine and finish off with a felt skull.

princess presents

Going home presents look extra special if they are prettily wrapped in a gathered circle of felt and secured with ribbons: fit for a princess.

post tepee

skill level **2**

time **4 hours**

you will need:

3 m (10 ft) pressure-treated round post, 15 cm (6 in) diameter

2 bags dry cement fixing

122 x 128 cm (48 x 51 in) marine plywood (or similar ready-cut size)

2 x 4.6 m (15 ft) lengths of rope, 1 cm (½ in) diameter

5 x 2 m (5 x 2 yd) fabric (see box on page 151)

sewing thread

6 m (20 ft) nylon cord

An alternative to the cocoon on page 134, this tepee set on a single leg is no less appealing. The improbability of the construction gives it instant child appeal and the opportunities for imaginative play are boundless. If you have more than one child and space allows, a small encampment of tepees would look even more enticing.

1 Drill two holes set at 90 degrees to each other, one just above the other, through the top of the post.

2 Dig a hole 70 cm (about 2½ ft) deep and just a little wider than the post. Lower the post into the hole and concrete around the post using the cement fixing in accordance with the manufacturer's instructions. Use a spirit level to ensure the post is upright. Leave the post-fix to cure overnight before continuing.

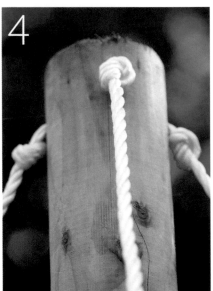

3 Use a 12 mm (½ in) drill bit to make a hole at each corner of the sheet of plywood. At the centre of the board, mark a hole large enough to pass snugly over your post. Cut it out with a jigsaw and lower the base over the top of the post.

4 Thread one piece of rope through each of the holes at the top of the post and pull each halfway through. Tie an overhand knot as close as possible to each side of the post.

5 Thread each end through the holes in the corners of the plywood. Tie overhand knots underneath the base so that it hangs level about 45 cm (18 in) above the ground.

6 Cut four large triangles of fabric, each 2 m (6 ft) tall, two with a base of 124 cm (50 in) and two with a base of 130 cm (53 in). Sew them together, small and large triangles alternately, to form a pyramid-shaped tent. Cut a slit halfway up one of the sides to form the door and hem the edges to stop them fraying. Now turn over a 2 cm ($^3/_4$ in) hem around the bottom edge of the tent, creating an open sleeve. Thread the nylon cord through this open sleeve.

7 Throw the tent over the post and draw the cord tight so the fabric is held firmly under the base and tie it securely. The tepee is ready for occupation.

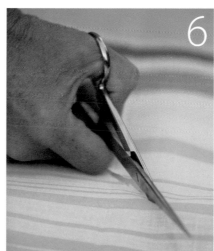

Choosing fabric

Sheeting cotton is ideal for this tepee, but if you can't find suitable fabric broad enough you could join widths together before you cut out, and even make a feature of bands of different colours. I cut all four triangles facing the same direction (see Step 6) to match up the stripes in the fabric I was using, but fabrics that don't need matching would take less if you cut your pieces as interlocking triangles as for the cocoon on page 134.

dinosaur footprints

skill level **2**

time **1 hour 30 mins**

you will need:
1 bag dry, mixed concrete

What could be more fun than following in the footsteps of a prehistoric dinosaur? Fossilized dinosaur footprint-style stepping stones are practical and make traversing the garden an adventure. Children can easily help with making these and will enjoy the messiness of the process!

1 First make your moulds. Dig several small holes in the ground about 30 cm (1 ft) wide and 10 cm (4 in) deep at the centre. (If you are cutting into grass, lawn turf can be replaced later if you cut it away neatly.) Use some of the soil you have removed to form the shape of a dinosaur footprint in the hole. Mould it into shape and compact it so it holds firm. If the soil is too dry add a small amount of water.

2 Mix up enough concrete to fill your moulds according to the manufacturer's instructions. Carefully fill each mould, gently agitating the mixture to help ensure all the spaces are filled. Leave the concrete to cure overnight.

3 Next day, gently ease your fossil stepping stones out of the soil.

4 Wash or brush off any soil from your dinosaur footprints.

5 Position the stepping stones in the garden, just far enough apart for children to be able to walk or jump from stone to stone.

QUICK & EASY IDEAS

LEFT Lush living willow can be used to weave dens large and small. The willow will sprout from cuttings or withies cut in the late autumn and winter and simply pushed into the ground. Their leafy greenness means the dens look at home in almost any garden and can even be set in a shrubby border. The maintenance is easy: just cut back or weave in the long arching branches each autumn. The simplest den to make is a tepee: push the withies into the ground (about 15–20 cm (6–8 in) deep should do) in a circle and tie them together at the top.

ABOVE Looking as if abandoned by pirates or highwaymen, this old tin trunk makes a practical, decorative storage solution for sand pit toys. It is worth giving what may be considered 'junk' a second look to see if it has potential.

RIGHT Heavy sleepers placed on the ground give just enough height to make a sand pit and a space large enough to accommodate a deckchair for the adults too. Place the sleepers on the ground, ends butted together, and line the area with thick plastic before filling it with play sand.

BELOW and BOTTOM RIGHT Boule is a game that can be shared by all the family. It may not be authentic but a large strip of sharp sand set in an area of lawn will be adequate for most families to enjoy the game.

QUICK & EASY IDEAS

RIGHT Give children a set of chalks and an expanse of decking or paving and the opportunities for play and artistic endeavour are endless: noughts and crosses, hangman, hopscotch, graffiti and all kinds of artwork. The slight anarchy of this activity always appeals. Always test the chalks to ensure they will not stain the surface you have chosen to draw on.

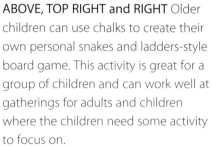

ABOVE, TOP RIGHT and RIGHT Older children can use chalks to create their own personal snakes and ladders-style board game. This activity is great for a group of children and can work well at gatherings for adults and children where the children need some activity to focus on.

RIGHT TOP and BOTTOM RIGHT
'Painting with water': quirky as it
sounds, this hot weather activity is
always a hit with young children. Give
them a bucket of water, an adult-size
paint brush and let them 'paint'
anything they want outside – patterns
on paving and walls, fences or objects.

LEFT Its seagoing days over, this
charming boat has come ashore to
provide a play feature in a family
garden. Set thoughtfully in the garden
the boat is a great prop for
imaginative play.

INDEX

ACKNOWLEDGEMENTS

My thanks to:

Clive Nichols for his matchless photography, tireless good humour and much valued friendship.

Harriet, Nancy, Joshua, Marlie, Clara, Josh, Ella, Yvette, Carragh, William, David, Gertie, Percy and Clive for their patience, posing and winning smiles.

All at Hamlyn, especially Sarah Ford and Emma Pattison, for making the book a reality.

Caroline Ball for her diligent and wise editing.

My parents for all their help, support, being utterly dependable and always having just the right styling props!

Peter Wheeler for his superlative carpentry skills and wise advice that saved me from a difficult situation. The tree platform, mobile fruit screen and criss-cross chairs would have been nothing without you!

Philip Smith for so ably stepping into the breach at the eleventh hour.

David Foster and Dougie Douglas for their heroic efforts with a difficult task.

The Gordon family for allowing me to plant up part of their garden.

Ropeloft for the prompt supply of fantastic rope (www.ropeloft.co.uk).

Executive Editor Sarah Ford
Editor Emma Pattison
Executive Art Editor Mark Stevens
Designed by Beverly Price, One2Six Creative Limited
Senior Production Controller Manjit Sihra
All projects created and styled by Clare Matthews

PICTURE ACKNOWLEDGEMENTS

Special Photography: © Clive Nichols
Other Photography:
Clive Nichols/Chapman Byrne-Daniel/Tatton Park 2002 97 top left; /David and Marie Chase's Garden, Hampshire 154 right, 155 top; /Robin Green/Ralph Cade 95 top left, 125 top; /Highfield Hollies, Hampshire 127 centre right; /Sarah Layton 154 left; /Stainton & Morgan/Westonbirt 2002 125 bottom; /Swinton Lane 66 centre left; /Trevyn Mcdowell 95 bottom left.
Octopus Publishing Group Limited/Stephen Conroy 32, 43 top, 43 bottom.